Can
on my
Resumé?

Strategies
that
WIN

The
Career Game

M. Rose Jonas, PhD
TV's Job Doctor

To David,
with the highest hopes you'll
follow your true path.

This publication is designed to provide accurate and authoritative information in regard to the subject matter covered. It is sold with the understanding that the publisher is not engaged in rendering legal, accounting or other professional service. If legal advice or other expert assistance is required, the services of a competent professional person should be sought. From a Declaration of Principles jointly adopted by a committee of the American Bar Association and a committee of Publishers.

"When I Was One-and-Twenty." From "A Shropshire Lad," Complete Poems, A. E. Housman. Used by Permission. The Society of Authors, London.

Printed and bound in the United States of America.
08   07   06   04   5   4   3   2   1

ISBN: 1-930500-16-5
Library of Congress Control Number: 2003115124

Cover design: VIP Graphics, (314) 535-1117
Published by: EFG, Inc., St. Louis, MO; (314) 762-9762

Distributed to the trade by:
Betterway Books
an imprint of F&W Publications
4700 E. Galbraith Rd.
Cincinnati, OH 45236
tel: (800) 289-0963 *fax:* (513) 531-4082

Your Game Plan:

1: Figure It Out

2: Go For It

3: Get the Job

4: Do the Job

5: Get Ahead

6: Get Out of Career Jail

7: Leave the Job

 # 1: Figure It Out, 13

2: Go for It, 48

What will help me narrow my focus?

Who can help me?

What am I willing to do?

What if I'm ready for something completely different?

How do I network?

What if I still don't have a vision of what I want to be when I grow up?

3: Get the Job, 83

4: Do the Job, 129

5: Get Ahead, 156

6: Get Out of Career Jail, 176

7: Leave the Job, 190

START Here

Watch Those Arrows

I sank into my new corporate chair behind my new corporate desk in my best corporate suit (also new). My high-potential smile was still plastered on my face because I'd forgotten to remove it when I'd closed my office door. It was my first day on the job as a junior executive. I was afraid and clueless.

How do things work around here? How do you figure it out? Who gives you good advice, and whose advice will land you in Career Siberia? How do you learn the rules of the corporate political game (and does it always move so fast, and did I already hear the thud of a political arrow in my new corporate briefcase as I walked down the hall)?

Who can I ask?

Today, as television's "Job Doctor," I know. But back then, I decided I didn't know anyone *inside* the organization well enough to trust with questions. No one *outside* corporate life understood it, so I floundered around—still smiling and faking it—believing I was hopeless and that everyone else knew what time it was.

I learned later about the wisdom of questions and picking mentors and how to hone your political senses and how commonly shared my confusions were. Along the way, however, I experienced numerous Machiavellian arrows in my ambitious posterior. I wasn't even smart enough sometimes to recognize the target painted there.

Painful experiences teach the most, often leaving the newly recovering with the resolve to turn back and lend a hand to others similarly struggling. My early days in the organizational trenches still carry the taste of fear and blood. They have created in me one of two passions which have since defined my career, and that is to show people how to navigate their career rapids, whether they're just venturing into the stream or bouncing off of the rocks. I'm an experienced boatman. I know how to get them through.

The other passion is a desire to level the work playing field, to even the odds in a game that always favors of the employer, "empowerment" jargon notwithstanding. Power plays. Demagogues. Dirty tricks. People treated like so many lower ranked pieces in the company chess game. Bosses behaving badly because they can get away with it. These are the coins of the realm in organizational life. Employers sometimes don't play fair, even when they want to do that. Few people know how to make you effective in the face of those lousy truths. I do.

I teach my clients how to be better engineers on their career track. Oh, you may still get fired or demoted or outplaced—I never claim the ability to step in front of and stop a screaming locomotive. But the company punches your ticket differently when you are a more canny driver. That's what I teach people to be.

So what is this book? *Can I Lie on My Resume?* answers the questions I had while quaking in my shiny new corporate boots. These are the career problems I've helped people solve, the answers I give viewers as "TV's Job Doctor." Chapter 1 helps you think about what career or job you want.

Chapter 2 tells you how to network and go for the job. Chapter 3 takes you through the interview process, from first phone call to the dilemma of taking a job you don't want. Chapter 4 joins you on your first day on the job, and shows you how to make a good impression and do a good job. In Chapter 5, you'll learn how to get ahead; in Chapter 6, how to get out of career trouble; and in Chapter 7, how to leave a job when you're finished with it, or it with you.

In each chapter, I raise the questions clients ask me, then give you the "winning strategies" and "The Point," your take-away learning. Start where you are in your career. If you're having trouble at work, flip to Chapter 6. If you're trying to decide what you want to be when you grow up (that's where people have the most work to do), start with Chapter 1. Think of this as a career reference book, with something to say to you at each point of the career game. Come back to it as you need it.

All career professionals have the same wish for you: Do what you love. Follow your passion. Be willing to put time and money into following your dream. Be patient - this takes awhile. My counsel comes from a "been there, probably already screwed that up myself" perspective. This book is like CNN's "Get to the point news." You have a question. The answer is here. I hope it makes you feel as if you're sitting across the desk from me, getting EXACTLY the career advice you need.

Can I Lie on My Resume? won't answer all your concerns. This is the first in a series of "career question" books. If you'd like me to answer yours in Volume 2, email me at (jobdoc@aol.com or use the form in the back.

When I ease myself into the chair on the news set to advise viewers about their career concerns, I sit on many arrow scars, some of which still make me wince. But they make me smarter on your behalf. I want you to succeed better, faster, more often than I did because you have answers to your most vexing career questions.

Pull up a chair and ask the Job Doctor!

CHAPTER
1

Figure It Out

How do I figure out what I want to be when I grow up?" This is the main question among many that clients ask. Should you be looking for something you're good at or that would make you happy? You've obsessed about the right career for months; why do you feel no closer to an answer? If you don't know what the jobs are or what they take, how can you pick one? How long does this take? What if you pick the wrong path?

Choosing a career puts you in your soul's center; you don't know the terrain or how to traverse it. You can work hard and not move a psychological inch closer to illumination. The two keys to career discovery are:

1. You MUST sit down and figure yourself out (no person or test can do that for you).

2. You MUST take action toward a goal, however fuzzy it will seem to you at first.

Whether you work through a book or a career counselor, do your career-pondering work like Cher does her exercises, "in the morning, so you don't have to worry about it the rest of the day." Set action goals each week. Make yourself accountable to someone else for taking action. Get going and keep moving.

The winning strategies in this chapter will help you begin.

How can I decide what I want to be when I grow up?

Winning Strategy #1:

Do What Curly and Mitch Tell You.

Remember the movie, "City Slickers"? Mitch (Billy Crystal), has just celebrated his 39th birthday. He feels lost and trapped in his job of selling radio advertising. His friends Ed and Phil drag him on a vacation trip to a New Mexico cattle ranch. For two weeks they'll play cowboy with real gauchos driving a herd to Colorado.

The city slickers' trail boss is Curly (Jack Palance), whose gruff ways keep everyone—cowpokes and cattle—in line. Mitch causes a stampede with his automatic coffee grinder, and Curly drags him out to round up strays. As they ride, Curly listens unsympathetically to Mitch fretting about life. He pulls his horse up.

"Do you know what the secret of life is?" he asks Mitch.

"No, what?"

"This," Curly replies, holding up one gloved finger.

"Your finger?" Mitch wonders.

"One thing, just one thing," Curly tells him. "You stick to that and everything else don't mean shit."

"That's great," Mitch says, "but what's the one thing?"

"That's what you gotta figure out."

It's the kind of response we often get when we take our confusions to a wise person. Their elliptical advice only confuses us more. "Thanks," we think, "I feel so helped."

Curly's right. You DO have to figure it out, largely because everyone else knows only a piece of you, and they'll almost never have your answer. You'll take a lot of wrong turns before you realize how unhelpful most of the advice-givers were.

The three city slickers soon find themselves as the only cowboys left to bring in the herd, and they decide to take on this impossible job. Of course they succeed. Just before they head back to their city lives, Mitch tells his friends he's figured out what Curly meant, what the "one thing" was.

"It's different for everyone," he tells them. "It's whatever's most important to you."

Sit for a bit and look at your finger to learn what that one thing is you're supposed to stick to. What's the most important thing to you? What captivates you? Has meaning for you? That which draws you also has the ability to energize, motivate and focus you, and RE-energize you when the going gets tough.

Curly and Mitch have some life instruction for you: The secret of life is to figure out what's most important to you. Do what Curly and Mitch told you.

Winning Strategy #2:
Find Your Mission and Vision.

W hy do you believe you were born? Why were you put on the earth? What do you believe you're expected to accomplish? What seems to pull you, drive you, meddle with your mind all the time? Work with these questions, and you will discover what gives your life meaning.

The answer may come readily: "To have children." For some, that completes the subject, which means they should organize their lives around this purpose. Work can be secondary for them. For others, even if having a family sounds purposeful, there's a sigh and a longing that tells me there's more they want to do in life, beyond work achievement or kids.

You may wrestle with life mission at age 20 or 60. If you keep the issue before you, you'll steer toward your particular star: perhaps to heal bodies or hearts; teach women to be leaders; make beautiful parties; make people laugh; feed them; advocate for them.

What tugs your heart is where your mission lies.

Your vision concerns what you want to achieve in life. It can be as grand as the companies you own, as fun as the adventures you intend to have before you get creaky and cranky, or as romantic as wanting to live near the shore. Vision covers everything. What kind of house do you want? When do you want to have children? Where will you send your kids to school? How much money do you want? When do you want to retire? What do you want to be doing ten years from now?

Not everyone likes this approach. They quote the old proverb: "Man plans, God laughs." They feel comfortable letting life unfold, living its moments and knitting a day-by-day life. They do not value a shrewd drive toward the so-called "right" direction. Knitting one's life does work. See what's here, scoop it up, work it into the pattern, appreciate the tapestry you're creating. It requires trusting, staying aware and being in the present. Even so, you should occasionally cast a glance outward when clouds form on the horizon.

You may like a more linear approach. Developing your vision clears away mental cobwebs and smoothes the path ahead of you. A friend once told me: "Make a list of everything you want to do in life—work-related and non-work-related—the 5 or 6 or 10 or 1000 things you want to do before you die. They can be pragmatic or outrageous; bold or quiet. Use that master list to shape shorter term goals, even daily to-do lists." If I want to climb a mountain by the time I'm 30, what should I be working on this year, this month, today? "Keeping the big list in front of you," he said, "will remind you where you want to go and the steps to get there."

It was difficult at first, then fun. I got as far as my next-year's list, tossed it in a drawer and forgot about it. It surfaced months later; to my surprise, by simply crafting the goals, I'd achieved about half of the things there. What might I have accomplished, had I kept this vision in front of me instead of under paperclips?

I'm a firm believer now in goal-setting. I regularly peer at the future's mists, boldly say, "This!" and "This!" and "This!" and march forward as if what I want is possible.

Working on your mission and vision will guide you, motivate you, help you understand where your interests do and do NOT lie. The task never ends; it changes as you change.

Try it. Take two pieces of paper. "Mission" goes at the top of one, followed by, "This is why I was born..." The mission is the BIG thing. "Vision" goes on another, followed by, "This is what I see for myself, what I'd like to have or achieve". The vision contains the dreams, achievements and activities. They need to support each other, but you may not immediately see a link.

On each sheet write anything that comes to mind. Get frustrated. Put it away. Come back to it. Try again. Once you realize your mission, you'll apply it in everything you do. You'll want it carved on your tombstone when you die, so people know you lived what you were here to do. Mine is "to make a difference in people's lives." What's yours? Regarding visions, these may be as solid as a bridge abutment or as wispy as cotton candy melting on your tongue. The "mission" list will give you a sense of why you're here, the "vision" what you want to make happen in life.

 **Let mission and vision guide you in your career decision-making and in your job search. You'll be glad you took the time.**

Winning Strategy #3:
Live your Life on Purpose.

T he closer you get to 40, the clearer your sense of mission might be. It may begin in general terms, like: "Help others" or "Teach young children." It may leap out at you like: "Help teenagers get off drugs," or "Write romance novels," or "Stop wastefulness in government." With or without a noble, heroic aspect, it will FEEL right and desirable to you.

As you continue to ask yourself "purpose" questions, the sense becomes stronger and details may emerge: "I'm here to teach and inspire adolescents in math." "My purpose is to make communities better." "I want to help poor kids become more financially knowledgable and independent." "I'm good at managing companies, and they need somebody like me if they want to grow."

If you will decide to live every day on your purpose—however haltingly you know what that is at first—you will be led in small-step ways to your larger mission. Within weeks (but sometimes months), you'll be willing, maybe eager, to venture into areas you hadn't considered. You may feel you're still not sure of the answer, but you'll know whether this is the right direction.

After awhile you may even be able to attach a job title and/or name of a desired industry. Your determination will be stronger than you ever imagined, even enough to overcome significant fears or barriers. Going through this process brings answers that come from the deepest part of you, where your unique meaning lies (and only YOUR meaning matters). You will hear and attend to your inner voice and ignore the external voices tuning up to discourage you, and you will find YOUR way.

There is almost never a direct path to your somewhere, but thoughtful moments spent alone and a decision each day to live on purpose will take you to awesome new places. "If I'm living ON MY PURPOSE, what will I do today?" You will create a powerful to-do list, as well as a "don't-do" list. If it's not on your purpose, why would you do it?

Try it. See if it doesn't clarify your priorities.

Winning Strategy #4:
Be Like Zusia.

You have a bundle of talents that make you uniquely you. What will you do with them?

Reb Zusia was a rabbi who lived in Poland just as the 19th century was dawning. He was a gentle, kind and caring teacher. One day his students, seeing his stricken face, asked what had frightened him.

"I have just had a vision of my death," he whispered. "The Almighty was about to pass judgment on me."

"You're a holy man, Zusia," they said. "Why would you tremble?"

"I knew I had to give an accounting of my life," he replied. "The heavenly court was not preparing to ask why I had not been great like Abraham, or a leader like Moses or a victor like Joshua. They were about to ask why I had not been like Zusia. THAT'S the question I fear."

You've heard this "days' end accountability" story in at least one other way, in the New Testament, when the master asks his servants what they'd done with the talents (money) he'd given them. Like Zusia and the good servant who was rewarded for tending well his master's affairs, you probably think sometimes about dying and standing before a celestial being who's flipped open a Book of Judgment to the page with your name on it. How much wound up in the debits column and will your credits cover them?

Your life accounting will cover more than whether you were naughty or nice. The question will be: What did you do with your talents?

Many of us spend our lives doing what we're SUPPOSED to do, sacrificing our gifts on the altar of "Making a living," or "My family needed me." I don't believe you'll get credit if you push your gifts, your essential YOU into a plastic bag and shove them under your bed, only dreaming about how you might bring them to life.

If you have the ability to carve beautiful tables, if wedding cakes leap exquisitely from your touch, if you can sell ice to Eskimos, you won't get an "Attaboy" if you didn't find in life a way to do that. You'll get an indignant, "Why didn't you use what I gave you? Why weren't you like YOU?"

This isn't necessarily a directive to ditch your job or your family to go write plays in a cold-water flat in New York; but take a brutally honest look at your life. If the essential YOU is suffocating in plastic, you may not be behaving like a noble, self-sacrificing heroine of a romance novel. You may be doing your distasteful jobs badly or bitterly, essentially punishing those around you because YOU decided you couldn't be YOU.

 You have gifts and the obligation to use them. Learn what they are and put them to work. Remember that debit/credit ledger and imagine what lengthy response you'd like to give at the Pearly Gates when you're asked, "What did you do with the gifts I gave you?"

**Where do you start,
if you want to make a career change?**

Winning Strategy #5:
Take the Time.

Clients seldom ask how long this career change process will take. Their impatient faces telegraph the hope we'll finish this in a jiffy.

How long does it take to choose or change a career? A handful of times a client, on a first visit, has leapt up with a "Eureka!" insight, given a tearful hug and bolted into the sunshine, inspired to start her own business, or parlay his academic career into an industrial specialty, or leave selling security systems for furniture refinishing. It is awesome to witness the birth of a new and strong career dream instantly to be pursued; memorable, too, because of its rarity.

Occasionally, the client makes a career change the ONLY item on his agenda, making career planning his work week, or stalling the job search process so that full time attention is first paid to the next career. In those cases, he makes it in three to six months. For most people, though, busy with job and family, it takes two years to dredge around in their attic of dreams and find the next path. This is intense work. How do you set aside the time when life's treadmill hums from dawn till midnight collapse each day?

This is also a numbers game. You have to make contacts, participate in activities, do research, write cover letters. The more you do, the faster you get through the process. It's an action game as well. You are seriously working when you're writing, phoning, meeting, or otherwise putting yourself on Front Street.

Clients protest when I tell them they're not doing what they should: "Oh, man, I think about this all the time!" Thinking gets you nowhere except whirling in the same mental circle. WRITE out your confusions, your goals, your networking list; PHONE for the class catalogue, the breakfast, the interview; MEET with the friend of a friend who does what you want to do; GO to the free seminars, the fall fest, the business-card-sharing cocktail parties; DO something every day in service to your career quest. (Pushier thinkers will tell you to do three to five things; and I think they're right. I've just never seen anyone DO it, unless they're on an actual job hunt. One thing a day seems to be challenging enough.)

"I can't wait that long," a client will often say; but then keep me along as coach on the struggling journey. At its end, 18 to 24 months later, I get a rueful, "You were right." It couldn't have happened any sooner; even the frustrations were valuable. One client passionately wanted to work for a specific big company, and we were both puzzled that he didn't get snarfed up by the business that truly needed him. Several months later he took another job that gave him big challenges and high visibility, just what he wanted. A few weeks after THAT, his first preference, Jumbo Co. announced massive layoffs. Whew. He'd found a better job AND dodged a downsizing bullet.

 A career change takes time. Set up your space; pick the time of day you do your best work; get out the address book or the contact program; organize the paper and pens and the "Do not Disturb" sign, and get busy. Two years will pass whether you work on this or not.

Winning Strategy #6:

Perform on Your Career Stage.

How you approach your career is influenced by where you are now IN your life. Are you just beginning? Are you surrounded by "little nose miners," as Mrs. Doubtfire called children? Do you gaze hypnotically at the gold retirement watch swinging before you? Psychologist Erik Eriksen called them the stages of one's life. I call them "career stages;" they have an enormous impact on what you'll be willing to do.

I outline elements of the stages here by age, but please take this as guideline rather than gospel. Folks like to plough a unique field. The guy who retires at 50 may start a new career at 60. The 42-year-old may never have had a setback or a younger boss or a terrifying night in a hospital with a sick child and felt his entire work-value system change. What follows is GENERALLY where people's heads are at a certain age. You only have to sit next to the 25-year-old who's retired in place to know that these career stages are as much a state of mind as distance from birth.

1. High school. Here's how people feel at this age: "I like hanging out. School is boring. I wonder, if I put it off long enough, my mom will fill out my college applications. Career? I just want outta this house!"

2. College. "I know enough that I have to do stuff that looks good on the resume. How can I make intra-mural couch-hugging look like a prestigious internship? What kind of job can you get if you're a liberal arts major? Graduate school. Wow, everybody's getting an MBA! Production management is boring, but I intend to go for the big bucks. Look at all that competition!"

3. First job. "I didn't go to school this long to do all this scut work. I'm not sure I like this place. When do I get the marketing job the brochures promised? I thought I'd have figured it out by now. Why am I not in charge?"

4. The ambitious years. After a few years in the trenches at a couple of jobs, we get focused. We're cool and making money. Our deodorant never fails. We get married. We have babies, and life takes on new meaning.

5. The changing years, which begin in our late thirties. Life has taken shape. We begin to examine it, especially if we haven't started a family and our life is pretty much our choice: "Did I pick the right career? I wish I knew what would make me happy." This is a big time for confusion and questioning the path we've taken, and for career change.

6. The mid-forties is another career change time. We've experienced death or illness among family and friends. We start to get what we're about and maybe what our mission is. We've been passed over and are no longer the Young Turks we thought we were. "I want to do something more meaningful." We go back to school. Community and where we came from matter now.

7. In our fifties our eyes are on the clock and our mortality. We want to live more on our own behalf and make a contribution. If we've been a good do-bee with our nose to the grindstone, this is the time we might follow our heart: Open a craft shop, teach, become a lay minister, leave the cog-job huge company to be important at a small one, take early retirement, get downsized and force ourselves to find something we want.

8. In our sixties we hit a desert. We're done, many of us. We are who we are. Our values have shifted to family and health, that book we always wanted to write, the time off we've neglected

to take. We know profound things, but others see our bodies (and too often our minds) as old. We are able and effective, but if we're unhappy at work, we pine to go. We emerge from this sojourn determined to: Do nothing. Or, start a new career, or get another job because we need or want to. Travel. Play endless golf. Dote on the grandchildren. Make our play our work.

9. As more 60- and 70-year-olds re-enter or never leave the work force, health, need and desire forge new career lives for people who reside in what Charles Handy called "The Third Age," the post-job era.

You can take a swing at any of the stages. Tell me about the career that never got off the ground, the bright star that faded young, the 40-year-old woman who began her career after raising her family, the 65-year-old nurse who joined the Peace Corps. Nonetheless, the life stages have different goals and fragrances . We WON'T be as ambitious and energetic at 60 as we were at 20. There's a time when "lookin' good" is primary, and another when "mission" drives us.

How old are you? What have you already accomplished? What are you up for? What (like dependent children or frail parents) MUST you consider? Do college-bound children keep you polishing your golden handcuffs? How far off is freedom? If your goal is to have children, what should you be doing NOW to build a career? How much flexibility do you have? How willing are you to wait for your dream?

Your questions matched with your career stage will help you to map your life along a line, beginning with now and headed toward a different age. What concerns you NOW? What will you be five or ten years from now? On a piece of paper, write today's year in the upper left hand corner. Pick a year, five or ten from now. Put that date in the upper righthand corner. Down the left side of the page, make a list of you and who's important to you, then any goals or dreams you have right now. The list might look like this:

Short Term Life Line	
This Year	Five Years from Now
Me—37	
Customer Service Manager	
Spouse—39	
Real estate agent	

Kids:
    Amber (5)
    Jake (3)	

Mom—67	

Goals
    College for kids
    One more baby
    Start my own business
    Get a bigger house	

Now for each line, mentally march across the next 5 years. What's likely to happen that could affect today's decisions? For example, if you're 37 and want another child, how long can you afford to wait? If you want to start a business, is the time ideal or terrible to have an infant? Which partner's job must have benefits? Is your mom independent and healthy now? How will your life change, relative to hers?

the Point

We can't predict life's path; but clients do get major "ahas" from seeing how much of their own life stage goes hand-in-hand with career decisions.

How do I know what's right for me?

Winning Strategy #7:

Don't Do What Your Parents Tell You.

"Telecommunications," his parents had hissed to him. "Huh?" I reacted to this college freshman who was clearly destined for the life of the Academy. Dead languages fascinated him. Dark, complex authors made his heart sing but sent his classmates to Cliff's Notes. He loved smoky, late-night debates over fine philosophical points. He wanted a Ph.D. so he could step into that most political ring...higher education.

His parents were loving, smart, attentive, and off the mark about their son. He was on that life trajectory a kid hits when he's 16 and swoops past well meaning but clueless parents left spinning in babyhood's dust.

Parents are my job security. They see newscasts about hot jobs and high salaries. They resurrect their own cold dreams from roads not taken and urge them upon the children. The urgings come from their deepest wishes: "Do better than I did. Don't stumble around as I did. Be 'possibilities' instead of 'settling'." They tout telecommunications, computers, finance, law; when their child is meant for sales, store management, teaching. It's made worse because the teen (typically unsure, unaware and undirected) believes the parent knows, and so begrudgingly takes the LSATs.

To this point the parents have said, "Do as I tell you." Now they should say, "What do you WANT to do?" and throw the teen into the cold terrors of life decision-making. They don't understand this child's heart anymore and they've forgotten their own resentment at parental nudging. So, they dictate to the teen who too often follows, then winds up in my office ten years later, a miserable dentist, lawyer, computer programmer, with money in the bank and misery in the heart. I ask the questions they should have struggled with years ago: "What do YOU want?" "What feels right for you?" The answer often suggests a dramatic change, to not-for-profit executive director, social worker, nurse. They become happier because they look into their hearts and decide.

Don't do what your parents tell you. Do what YOU tell you. Begin at your insecure base and build a confident foundation that results from constantly asking, "What do I want?" "What feels right for me?" Because parental teachings go deep, it may take time to get to the real you.

You have to train your instinct just as you train your body for a 5K run. You must decide—because people will never stop telling you what to do with your life—what feels authentically you. Start asking yourself those two key questions today. Let it take the years it requires to hone a keen sense. Hope for a clear memory of your own struggle when, twenty years from now you're tempted to hiss "space station management" into your own child's adolescent ear.

 **Do what matters to you.**

Winning Strategy #8:
Make Yourself Happy.

Too many of us have no idea what would make us happy. We've trained ourselves to look toward the world for what's supposed to make us happy. We chase something (the new car, the fountain pen, the cool job), only to find in its capture, "Nope, that wasn't it."

Your inner self has probably hammered to be heard, but the noise of your "gotta-shoulda-woulda" train drowns out that voice. To find out what would make you happy, listen for its quiet longings.

What does that have to do with your job? We bring a multitude of values and capabilities, quirks and desires to work. If the work satisfies them, we are fulfilled in our career. It's more than deciding you want to be a FILL-IN-THE-BLANK. It includes these puzzle pieces as well:

1. What do you want to be? Do you have a name for your career? Doctor? Teacher? Physical Therapist? Financial advisor? People rarely know, though at mid-career they often want the long-held dream they denied themselves at the beginning: the doctor who'll become a minister, the lawyer who wants to be a psychologist, the carpenter who wants to make defense maps. If you don't know, that's okay. Many of us never find an ideal THING to say we are. Who, after all, says, "Gosh, I'd just die to be an administrative drone!" Yet a lot of us become that, and we find a measure of happiness surrounded by administrivia. We may only uncover what we call ourselves for the moment: a commercial lender, a marketing manager, an operations director. In five years, maybe we'll be something else.

2. What kinds of problems do you want to solve? What subject matter fascinates you? What are you ALWAYS interested in, no matter what? Are you fascinated by interiors? Making figures mean something? Writing speeches? Learning everything there is to know about law in the 17th century? Making communities better?

3. What processes do you love? Becoming an expert, no matter the subject? Making an organization run smoothly? Shaping things with your hands? Making other people look good? Making the sale? Coming up with diagnoses? Solving puzzles?

4. How do you want to work with people? Alone or on a team? What kind of people do you want to be around all day? Creative? Smart? Regular guys? Unconventional? Ambitious? In need of you?

5. What work environment appeals to you? A small office with lush green plants? A large corporation with long, clean hallways? A loft building in the heart of the city? A peaceful suburban setting close to your home? A manufacturing plant? A loading dock? A cozy cubicle? A corner office? Your basement?

6. What in your personal life has an impact on work? Do you have young children? Do you want to work close to home because of your family or just because you don't like long commutes? Is your spouse in school? Are you likely to move frequently?

Be creative in coming up with your answers. Do this in a place where your mind can roam, your body can be comfortable. Put it on a blackboard or chart paper. Use markers or water colors. Get to the heart of what makes you happy, and the world's insistences will rattle you less.

How to work with this: Take a sheet of paper for #1 "What do I want to be?" Jot down what you're considering. Take another sheet for #2, "Problems I want to solve." List them. Repeat for each number. Any inspiration? Ideas? Conclusions? If yes, how can you start working towards this career in earnest? If no, put it away for a bit. We'll be looking at this again.

 Make yourself happy. The day is too long to be unhappy in it.

Winning Strategy #9:
Make a Refrigerator List.

This is similar to the "make yourself happy" list, but it invites people from your world to participate. Author and professional speaker Carol Weisman developed the Refrigerator to figure out her next career. She had been a medical social worker and knew it was time for a big change. She'd spent years working from her heart with patients and with volunteer organizations, but she needed to make a better living. She put three headings on a piece of paper:

1. Absolutely Must Have
2. Preferences
3. Absolutely Not

What were the MUSTS for her next job? Travel, independence, the ability to make money were a few. What were her PREFERENCES in a job, not deal-breakers, but nice to have (some travel, make my own hours)? And finally, what could she ABSOLUTELY NOT tolerate, whether it was a subject matter, a responsibility (like filing or bookkeeping), a condition (not having a boss)?

She taped the list to her refrigerator and left it there for months, jotting down things as they occurred to her, inviting family and friends to suggest dazzling personal talents she might have left out. "What do I look like to you?" she'd ask. One day a friend studied the sheet, "hmmmed" and said, "You're an independent business woman who specializes in working with not-for-profit boards, who writes books and gives speeches." Voila! A new and highly successful career was born. Carol is now a keynote speaker, and she wrote five books on board development in her first seven years as president of her company, Board Builders.

You may not be as lucky to have a friend put it all together for you. But use Carol's technique to get you started. Make the list. Hold it on the fridge with those attractive vacation magnets you've collected, and see what comes up for you and others.

Learn what matters to you in a job so you'll know what you're looking for besides its title and perks.

Winning Strategy #10:
Get in the 'Way Back Machine.

This tip scoops up your childhood memories and sifts them for clues to your today's mysteries.

Surf the cable channels and you'll find "The Adventures of Rocky and Bullwinkle," a cartoon series from the late 1950s. One of the segments had an intellectual dog, Mr. Peabody, and his young bespectacled assistant, Sherman. They would board their "'Way Back Machine" and travel back in time for a fractured look at history. Since the piece was often a long set-up to an outrageous pun, you wouldn't win Ben Stein's quiz show money if you rattled off any factoids picked up on your trip with Peabody and Sherman.

If you traveled in your own 'Way Back Machine to your kid years, however, you might learn a great deal about yourself, because what you were doing THEN holds valuable clues to what would make you happy NOW. Ready? Create a mental image of you when you first remember yourself at play...age 5, 6, 8. Let your childhood playtimes parade before you like a movie, up to your adolescence. What intrigued you, kept you fascinated for hours? Take notes as you "watch" your movie. When the final credits have rolled over your dawning adulthood, look at what you've written.

Do you have a book of mementos from your early years? Report cards? Scrapbooks? Treasured toys? Haul it out of the basement. What does this mini-architectural dig suggest for your career? Is there a remembered voice of a favorite teacher who believed in you?

Your childhood fascinations hold profound insights for making today more gratifying. The meaning you give your play is key. If you loved to read, maybe that's all it meant. It could also signify you'd be successful going on to advanced degrees, working in a secondhand book shop, doing research. People who were fascinated by puzzles might like consultancy or jobs requiring analysis. Kids with short attention spans and high energy levels can become entrepreneurs or surgeons or TV producers, but not desk-sitters. The outcast writes dark novels, the dreamer crafts poetry, the blocks-obsessed become sculptors, architects, geometry teachers.

The processes of thought, movement or observation that captivated you THEN hold a key to what will make you happy NOW. You might even see how your life has tried to live up to your childhood play. You were Snow White in the first grade pageant; today, you're a trainer. You always played "grocery store;" today, you have a food business. You had to be in charge; now you own a company.

Show your list to other people. What do these combinations of interests mean to them? When you ask, be prepared to get the "wrong" answer for you. That's okay. What feels wrong about it? Does "right" occur to you as a result? It often does.

 **Your 'way back past holds valuable clues about your future.**

Winning Strategy #11:

Pick Your Part in the Play.

In high school you auditioned for the role of romantic lead in the annual play, but got picked for the chorus. Bitter, you blew off rehearsals, lost the part and didn't even go to the play.

Show biz is tough, isn't it? Actually, everyone should have the experience of a professional audition: Getting up the courage to go, the agony of waiting, the terror of handing your music to the accompanist, being in mid-warble when a disembodied voice says, "Thank you," and you're shown the backstage door. There is no crueler reality check than to know your talent and looks had little to do with it. "You weren't the type we were looking for." If you'd been taller, younger, more Norwegian-looking...nothing you can control.

If you're smart, you learn what your type is and sell that instead of railing against casting directors for not being creative in their vision, not seeing past a type to consider the uniqueness of you. I mean this in the deepest and most fundamental sense. What ARE you anyway? Are you the lead? A character actor? A techie? A costumier? A casting director?

As you go through life, pay keen attention to what draws you. If you like performing, maybe sales or speaking or teaching are for you. If you like being the Number Two who makes Number Ones successful (you enjoy the work and love the sense of accomplishment, but don't like being the out-front person), then look at operations or administration or consulting.

Do you like working with words or abstract ideas? Do you love digging out facts or presenting them? Those desires and preferences are clues to the PROCESS of work that will make you happy. Don't try to understand it. Just accept it and put yourself in those places where you can do what you love about 80 percent of the time.

We get hung up in our early years trying to convince ourselves and others that we want to be the star of the play. There's only one lead, but dozens of other roles abound. If you step bravely into the one that feels most like you, you'll find an instant contentment. The star thing is what you're supposed to want. Go for it if that's you, but if you admit in some bleak midnight hour that you're a stage manager or a stagehand, a props mistress or lighting director, step into that role as quickly as you can.

You can bring star quality to any role you play. Just put yourself in the right one. You'll find it if you'll pay attention to what work processes bring you satisfaction.

Winning Strategy #12:
Go to a Party.

Imagine you're at a party. The guests are people you don't know but want to impress. No one from your family was able to show up, and you're glad—they have too many opinions! You're holding your glass of Chardonnay or diet soda or martini. The person next to you shifts to the "getting to know you" party patter.

"What do YOU do?" It's the question that always follows the greeting and name-sharing. You look the person in the eye and say…what? What do you hear yourself saying? If you're thinking about a career change, imagine you've made it already and give the name of your new career. If you're wondering if you'd like a particular job, tell the other guest this is what you do.

How did it feel to fill in the career blank? Were you proud to reveal your job and your company? Did you fudge because your company's controversial? Did the title fit you?

It's amazing the impact this simple exercise can have. One client who'd left a high powered job for a low-tech one she liked realized she felt unhappy because the prospect of party talk shamed her. She imagined what other people would think: "How could such a talented person be doing this? What's wrong with her?" She hadn't liked the bigger job, but she loved the rush she got telling others about her high-status job. Once she realized this was holding her back, we developed new party chatter for her.

This isn't about impressing party strangers, but getting a sense of how YOU feel about what you want to do, what you'd like to say about yourself or fear saying. You left your impressive company seven years ago, but still need to say at parties that you USED to be there. What's wrong with what you've been doing recently? What kind of status do you need to give yourself so you can drop your past like a bad habit?

If you play the party game and say with pride that you're a graphic designer or a mom (one woman said she was in "citizen development") or a marketing director or legal secretary, that's a big clue to where you and your life should be headed. Go to the party.

How do I keep myself motivated?

Winning Strategy #13:
Hire Me.

Warning: *Commercial ahead.*

You're miserable in your career. You've fussed over it for months. You've read the books, but you feel no closer to a solution. Think of doing this: Hire me! (or another career counselor/coach/life strategist/yenta) In fact, I wish people would get to this point sooner. Sometimes they're pretty beaten up by life's stormy waves by the time they fling themselves on my shore. I could've spared them a few bruises.

Some folks don't need assistance from others. They can read the manual and figure out the software program. Others feel distinctly uncomfortable showing their souls to another. The rest of us value having new eyes and heart on the problem. We move better and faster that way.

Some career companies charge thousands of dollars, so be sure you know exactly what the counselor will provide; and get references. Shop around to find the right helper and the right price.

Having done this work for years, I can see a connection between money and the attention the seeker will give to this life project. The person willing to plunk down the fee is usually also willing to do the serious work required, as if saying, "This is an investment in ME and I'm worth it and I intend to get my money's worth." She doesn't just dip a toe into the chilly career waters. She strides in like she has a job to do, cold water or not.

If you truly don't have the money for a coach and the books don't work for you, then think about these as options:

1. Your college. Universities often have free career programs for alums.

2. Community service job clubs or federally assisted programs. These are either free or low cost ($50 or less). They can be run by churches or have certain requirements, like being downsized, but they're there. Ask around.

3. Community colleges. Take the right number of hours and you'll qualify for their free student services.

4. Adult ed programs, often held in high schools. You can do these classes at night or on Saturdays. Call your school district to see who sponsors it. Also, about a $50 fee. The biggest problem with these programs is that they're public venues. You may not be willing to share your secrets with strangers, and this process usually requires openness.

With a career counselor, the focus is private and on you. The professional does this for a living, has probably met your problem already, along with the resistance and other blocks you might have, knows how this works, has the skill to pull or push you through, and is ethically bound to keep your life and path confidential.

How do you find one? The same way you find a doctor, a therapist, a babysitter. Ask your friends. If they give you good reports on a counselor or a program, check it out. If the counselor has written a book, read it. See if you like its philosophy. Go hear a speech. Could you work with this person? Schedule one appointment. Do you like the person, feel like you're in good hands, that she'll be a skilled guide on this journey?

Whatever feels right for you is right for you. I don't care if the person is billed as the best in the world and EVERYONE says is awesome, if he's not awesome to you, he's not awesome. You are the best judge.

What's the process like? It could be one-on-one sessions, involve testing or a months-long program. Everyone's different.

How much does it cost? You could pay nothing for a volunteer-run church program or up to $200 an hour for individual sessions. You could pay $50 for a Saturday workshop, or hear that an open-ended program will cost you $3,000. Make sure you're clear about the investment.

You are worth the money and the effort, and I hope you discover that.

 **Get the help you need.**

How do I bring all of my career pieces together?

Winning Strategy #14:
Finish the Quilt.

Think of you, your experiences and strengths as a patch-work quilt project. You are a collection of plaids and stripes, vibrant as well as dull color. None of it matches, but somehow the talented quilter can make these odd shapes and threads into something both useful and beautiful.

Let's make the "quilt." Take several sheets of paper, neon-bright or plain. At the top of each put a heading. Use one page for each topic of personal discovery you've made. They might have titles like:

- ❑ My Career Values
- ❑ My Mission: Why I Was Born
- ❑ Vision for Myself
- ❑ Major Life Goals
- ❑ Refrigerator List
- ❑ Geography Desires (or Limitations)
- ❑ Title I Want
- ❑ Fields that Fascinate Me
- ❑ Work Environment
- ❑ Work Processes I Love
- ❑ Problems I Want to Solve
- ❑ Money I Need to Make
- ❑ My Best Skills
- ❑ Dreams for Me
- ❑ Dreams for My Family

Your list could look exactly the same or quite different from this. The criterion for inclusion is that the topics or issues feel vital to you.

You'll notice that negatives will pop up; worries or problems that affect your career dreaming. In training classes, when the group brings up issues not part of the discussion, the facilitator entitles a flip chart "Parking Lot." The trainees "park" items that might sidetrack the seminar. You need one, too. You dream of going back to school. You worry about funds. Dump "funds" on the parking lot, along with all your big negatives. Stay mindful of them, because career dreams have costs and concerns to manage. But don't let them overpower the dream. First get the laser-sharp picture of where you're headed.

Got your notes? Got the parking lot? Sit at the dining room table. Put the parking lot 'way over to the side. Put all your dream notes into a square or circle. See how interesting you are, with all your dreams in one place? In the center put another sheet that says, "What does all this mean to me?" Carefully study each of the notes and write on the center sheet any discoveries or "ahas."

If you prefer big and bold, tape butcher paper to a wall or use a Dry Erase board. Think of the artist standing before a canvas, about to create. The mind and body flow into the work, through the artist's arms as well as eyes; the light that comes in the window AND the music playing on the radio. You are the artist of you. Put yourself into it. Get glue and markers, sparkles and string, and decorate your "quilt."

Like an artist, step back from your work and see what it says about you. Take time to understand your creation. Don't talk about it; rather, wait, so you know what REALLY feels like you. (Painters and writers often don't tell people much about their work in progress. They don't want outside influence. They're also easily discouragable. They need to concentrate on what THEY mean, not on what someone's thinks they SHOULD mean. The same is true for you in splashing yourself on the page. Until you breathe life into your art, you'll be too influenced by what others say. People love giving advice; too often, it has nothing to do with YOU, more what THEY would do if they could. Get a good sense of you-as-art before you go public.

NOW invite comment. Talk with friends who know you, who know the world, and can give you a perspective. Take in only what has meaning to YOU. YOU are the only entrant into this art fair and its sole judge. Everybody else is adjunct.

The answer lies before you. If you don't come up with answers right away, keep your pages prominently displayed and stare at them till enlightenment dawns. This won't be easy. You will want others to tell you. You will feel there's no answer for you, but I promise you - especially if you look at this as a puzzle you can solve - you'll come up with answers.

 You have been searching your heart for several weeks. Now bring all the pieces of you together. You may discover a name for your next job or career.

CHAPTER

2

Go For It

You have some clarity and, even if you don't have an exact name for your next job or career, you're ready to venture forth. How do you network? Who do you call? What do you ask for? How soon should you target decision-makers or start interviewing?

Taking you and your career dream on the road is just like making sales calls to get business. It's a numbers game, and the more fruitful contacts you make, the closer you'll come each time to knowing what you really want AND where your next job is. It takes courage, organization and a plan, but—as they say in Twelve-Step programs—"It works, when you work it."

What if you don't have the dream yet or can't leave where you are? There are no guarantees you'll reach the end of your soul's quest. I see clients do diligent work and still not come up with an answer. I don't know what stands between them and that "Let's roll" energy. They just stay stuck.

You may be deeply unhappy but lack the time or courage to make those networking calls. You may not be ready. Perhaps you have family obligations or need to heal from a horrible work situation. Maybe you're unwilling to make a move, not convinced your dream is real. Whatever the reason, please respect where you are, forgive yourself, put this down for a bit, go get the "just a job" or stay at the old one, and come back to the task later. You will NOT be ready till you're ready.

What will help me narrow my focus?

 Winning Strategy #15:
Write Me a Letter.

A powerful way to know what you want is to imagine yourself as actually living in one of your possibilities, and, from the perspective of BEING THERE in the future, contact us back here and tell us what you're doing and why you so successfully achieved that dream.

A client couldn't decide whether she wanted to be a pharmacist, dancer, or business manager. All three enticed her. "Write me a letter," I told her, "as if it's five years from now. Actually, write me THREE letters. In each one, pretend you've become one of these occupations. Tell me how you left our session and started on the pathway to become what you are now, a successful (fill in the blank). Tell me what you do all day and why you love it. How did you get here? What is there about you that's made you so successful? Why was this the perfect career choice?"

At our next session she handed me three letters, laughing. In the first she'd become a pharmacist and was depressed to report that she stood on her feet all day and counted pills. The second came from her as a ballerina, in which she reported the physical miseries of trying to force a 30-year-old body into the pretty balletic pretzels that are better learned young, and how she could see she was past her prime. The third letter went on and on about how she'd gone back to business school. She'd always enjoyed her family's dinner table conversations about its business; now she wanted to be part of it.

Tra la, and she was gone, off to the university admissions office to sign up for her MBA classes. This after having spent literally months stuck over those three dreams and not being able to take them anywhere.

This exercise brings you and your heart and brain together in a wonderful way. No one is with you to suggest or criticize. The reality is whatever you want it to be. It forces you to consider what you bring to the dream, whether you really believe you have the drive and determination to shape those wisps of confused desire, whether the excitement goes bone-deep. Are you truly willing to make the sacrifices going back to school will require? Did you realize that, to become a powerful attorney, your nanny would be raising your children? Do you understand that what you want to do means you must move from your pleasant little town to a mammoth city?

You'd be surprised how much you already know about your dreams. You just haven't taken the time to bring daylight to them. Ask someone to be the "recipient" of and commentator on your dream letters. Set a date by which you'll have them finished. Get to work. Write me a letter.

 **Act as if your career dreams have already come true.**

Winning Strategy #16:
Walk Through Peanut Butter.

Thanks to the magic of television sitcoms, we incorrectly believe:

1. Life proceeds in a linear fashion, with mostly laughs along the way and a tidy end, and

2. We can make things happen fast. If you look at your own life, however, you know it is not so. Relationships don't mend, people die before realizing a dream, and—especially if you've ever headed a committee—progress proceeds at a snail's pace. Life can be like herding cats. Sure, the laughs are there, but what a wild journey.

You've probably brought those two cultural beliefs to your career search and given yourself a hard time because you think that what you want should be crystal clear to you, and the path to the destination well defined. Even now, when you've spent so much GOOD time at this project, why are you still confused about next steps? Because you're supposed to be.

The only way out is *through*. You have to go through a career wilderness that feels like walking through peanut butter; dense, sticky, barely pushable. People try to skirt it because they want the end result—without the mess. They're surprised to find themselves stuck anyway. You just have to suck it up and march forward in what feels like the right direction, and you will find yourself on the other side. The gift for those efforts will be clarity.

Here's an example. What do you think you want to do? Find someone who does it and meet with her. Do you hate hearing about the hours or the travel or the pay, but something else in your conversation piques your interest? Ask her if you can talk with someone who does THAT. Meet with him, and check your gizzard to know how his career appeals to you, or not.

There's a saying that we're only six people away from anyone we need. It seems also to be true that we have to waste about six contacts not getting anywhere, like we're walking through peanut butter. Be patient and persistent through those six frustrating contacts, and I promise you'll get closer to what you really want which is, after all, the point of the exercise. Once you can definitively identify it, ANYONE can help you.

Make that first phone call, walk up to that house-sized blob of peanut butter, make your hands like a wedge, and push forward. Honestly, you'll be fine.

Don't forget the chocolate sauce! It makes a walk through peanut butter at least tastier.

 **Get going, even if you're not 100 percent sure where.**

Winning Strategy #17:

Think Before You Go to a Recruiter.

Clients always hope a recruiter holds the solution to their career dilemma.

Sometimes I daydream I'm getting an award from a national convention of executive recruiters. As I walk up to the dais, they rise as one, greeting me with deafening applause, wiping away tears of gratitude because I—with this Winning Strategy—persuaded job seekers to STOP CALLING THEM. Then the cold wind of reality whirls in the door with my client who asks, "Should I go see a headhunter?" Poof. Here comes another innocent with the desperate hope that a profession will operate quite differently than it does.

The question behind the question is, "Please tell me where I can find someone who will do the work FOR me so I don't have to do it." Who WOULDN'T want to walk into an office, plunk down a resume, smile and wave and walk out, secure in the knowledge some hard worker in the back will rush to the phone and start calling employers who just MUST know about this latest talent; then ring us up when that job interview is scheduled?

I don't discourage the recruiter visit. I also know the question is the last distraction before they realize this is hard work and it all sits at the CLIENT'S home address. They will come back with a drooping spirit but a willingness to finally settle in and do the real grind.

If you're a garden-variety worker, most recruiters aren't interested in you. They get paid BY EMPLOYERS between 10 and 35 percent of the hired recruit's first year's salary. Companies aren't interested in shelling out that money unless they can't find candidates on their own, or they're so rushed to make a huge hire or they don't have the staff to do it. Plus, most recruiters specialize in one or two or three things: computer programmers, creative people, human resource managers, CEOs. Their attitude is, as Annie Gray, principal of Annie Gray Associates, Inc. told me, "Don't call me. I'LL find YOU."

Their fees are called "contingency" (they get paid only if they find someone) or "retained" (they get paid for presenting qualified candidates). A few work on an hourly basis. There are others who ask the job seeker to pay a fee, usually several thousands of dollars: These are bottom feeders who go after the unskilled, unsophisticated, desperate or lazy job seeker, who seldom produce the desired result, though their hand is out for your ready cash.

Executive recruiters, in my experience, are nice people who love making the connection between candidate and job. That's why they'll interrupt their efforts to find a new customer or a candidate for an existing one, to ask you, "What kind of job are you looking for?" Steam comes out of their ears when the callers say—even highly intelligent types, "Gee, I don't know. I thought if I could look at the jobs you have, I could figure out which ones I'm qualified for." If you drop in, they'll take the resume and smile sweetly; but I assure you it hits the round file the second you go out the door.

The way THEY find YOU is to troll their sources: directories, former placements, friends, colleagues, source-filled address books, and the Internet (and, yes, they get annoyed when they place several ads on Monster.com and the same person applies for the Director of Engineering, the Comptroller and the Office Manager's job).

If you want to use a recruiter, do your work first. What kind of job are you looking for? Which recruiters specialize in what you do? Prepare your 20-second elevator speech so you show the recruiter you call that you know what you want and that you're respectful of her time. If you're a chemical engineer and the recruiter specializes in ChemE's, she may be genuinely interested in you.

The statistics are bleak about who gets a job through recruiters, but my personal gauge is that NONE of my clients have done so. You get your job through the grind of figuring out what you want, making networking calls, sometimes scouring the want ads and scrambling to get an interview. It ain't glamorous, but that's how it's done.

Go to a recruiter if you must, but only if you know what you want. Research the recruiter before you go; and when you come back.... let's get down to the real work.

Winning Strategy #18:
Get a Buddy.

P eople making a career change show a brave smile to the outside world, but in my office we talk about how difficult it is to make this change. Nearly everything they have to do takes courage: Call people you don't know. Dig around in your soul. Live in the uncertainty of not-knowing, over a possibly long period of time. Think you should know, but don't. Tell people how great you are. Ask for favors. (Ah! It feels like begging.) Decide what you want for the rest of your life and go for it.

We are not raised to be good at this. We resist. Put it off. Delay. Career changing is as dreadful as doing daily exercise. Yes it's good for us; but we prefer our warm blankie over the pain of dragging ourselves up and out. We're not stupid. Our systems tell us it's smart to go for pleasure and to avoid pain, and a lot of this is painful.

So, you sit like a frog on a log on a sunny summer's day. You should get moving but don't want to. There's no one to MAKE you, unlike the routine of your daily grind. You have to get up, you have to make the 8:10 a.m. bus to downtown, you have to pick up the kids from ball practice, you have to do the laundry. There's a lot in there you probably don't want to do, but you have a keen sense of I GOTTA DO THIS, and so you do.

With career musings, however, you can wait the rest of your life. There's no real pressure. Making yourself happy is a concept that may feel foreign to you. Delay, then, seems logical.

What do you do if you're miserable in place, can't seem to motivate yourself, and don't want to hire a career counselor?

Get a buddy! Set up an external accountability person, to whom you'll commit finishing specific tasks (write the resume, make five networking calls), someone you'll call on a regular basis (every week or two) to report your progress.

This is YOUR responsibility, so you must not make a buddy feel, "Wow, I've just taken on another job." The buddy only has to take your call and give you comments or encouragement, if that will help you. The point is to make yourself feel you HAVE to complete tasks. If you're training for a marathon, it's easier if you're meeting pals at the track at dawn than if you promise yourself you'll get out of bed a half hour earlier. (I'm a member of the Chaffing Dishes, an elite group of plus-size runners. I—Grumpy Spice—am grateful to the other Spice Girls—Lumpy, Gazelle and Sciatic Spice—they MAKE me come to the track.)

Whom do you ask? One client asked his sister to be his buddy after he'd spent a fruitless year trying to get a job in another city. He called her every Sunday night, telling her what he'd gotten done and made a commitment for the next week. He had another job within three months.

Meet a friend for coffee every week. Send an email report to your cousin in Dubuque. Find other friends in similar circumstance and form a loose federation of dream seekers and help each other.

 Career work is more easily done when another person helps.

What am I willing to do?

Winning Strategy #19:

Your "Want to" vs. "Will You."

As you pick your way across the minefield of decision, an idea leaps at you. "This could be for me!" you think. "I've wondered about...being a lawyer, a not-for-profit accountant, a social worker, a real estate developer, a recruiter." Behind the idea lie two diverging paths. Over one is an arch marked, "Want to" and over the other is, "Will you?"

You peek beyond the "Want to" arch. A pile of obstacles lies between you and the dream. On the sideline, someone (Parent? Spouse? Best friend?) mocks you: "You're crazy to do this at your age." "You'll never make money doing THAT." You see the mountains of work to be done, the whitewaters of risk to traverse. The cold winds of the solo journey swirl towards you.

This is the dream path, begun alone. Others can't see your vision and they're afraid for you. When you succeed, however, they'll recall having been your supporter. What blocks that path is the universe's test of your determination and is as predictable as afternoon rain in monsoon season.

Next to this is the "Will you?" arch and path; sunnier, smoother, more sensible. Friendly hands beckon you toward this easier way. Which path will you choose?

We dream of what we WANT to do, but we demonstrate the dream's strength by what we WILL do. Will we pay the money, give up the time, forgo vacations or family time, sustain despite criticism? Or will we back away, claiming commitments, lack of energy or time or resources? Whatever your reasons, they are powerful, and stop your action.

It's not bad, simply an indication that you wanted something else MORE right now. Dreams are flexible, persistent. You can often pull them out later when you're freer, braver, richer...or more determined.

 Your behaviors are the best proof of whether you're on the "Want to" or the "Will you?" path. If you're not taking any actions to get there—filled out the application, checked the web site, called for the brochure, made the appointment for the informational interview—then you're on the "Will you?" path. Put dreams aside and embrace today's decision. You know what's best for you. You also know where to find the dream when you decide "I WILL" replaces "I want to."

Winning Strategy #20:
Keep Your "but" out of It.

You want to quit. Legions of colleagues know the tortuous details of your dreadful boss, the work that's beneath you, the lousy assignments and pay, the lack of recognition. They rise to your bait giving you ideas, motivational talks and pats on the po-po.

You do nothing. Finally, your friends realize you're behaving like the frog in the Bugs Bunny cartoon who endlessly sings, "Hello my baby!" to his astonished owner. When he brings others to witness the incredible warbler, the frog sits—top hat lopsided on his head—and only gives out a froggy "Bruuup."

"Bruuup" shows up in your conversation as, "Yes, but. . ." For every creative idea others get of what you CAN do, you have a rock-solid reason why you CAN'T.

"You could go back to school."

"Yes, but I don't have any money." Bruuup.

"Maybe you could look for another job."

"Yes, but I work all day. I don't have the time." Bruuup.

This is you dancing away from taking responsibility for your own life. You prefer to place the blame on your pig of a boss or your mean co-workers.

the Point

If you hate your job, your environment, your salary, do something about it. Don't hide behind the economy, your age, your kids, your lack of time. It's your pond and whether you sing in it is up to you. Go for it and leave your "but" out of it. No Bruuups.

P.S. Sometimes you can't leave. See the "Choose Chicken" strategy, Page 81.

What if I'm ready for something completely different?

 *Winning Strategy #21:*
Check out the Entrepreneur Thing.

You sit in your cubicle, resenting everything and everyone. You chafe to be on your own. "Me, Incorporated." You like the sound of it.

Are you cut out to be an entrepreneur, a business owner? Do you have a product the market wants, or capital, or the skills to run a business? Many don't, and that's why 75 percent of new entrepreneurial businesses fail within two years. The wide-eyed and hopeful say, "Sure!" but the allure of "becoming my own boss" distracts them from taking a firehard look to be sure they have what it takes

Entrepreneurs have certain characteristics. Do you have them, or should that cubicle remain your corporate home?

1. What's your need for security? This is the pivotal and never-ending question. Lack of security is your reality on the first day in an entrepreneurial business...and on the ten thousandth. You'll always be the last one paid, and you can go for weeks without a paycheck. If you must have regular, predictable income and a benefits package, you'd better stay where you are.

2. What's your need for the water cooler? Entrepreneurship can be lonely. Organizations provide schmoozers and resources

(ideas, training, desks and pencils) and daily interaction. Can you be without those? To succeed, you'll have to set up pockets of mentors, schmoozers and idea people.

3. How good are you without structure? Yeah, I know you're totally independent in your job, but highly disciplined moguls stumble when they have to create their day from scratch. Most of us feel better within a structure. It's why 95 percent of us work for others.

4. Do you have a cash reserve to cover 18 months of your family expenses in case the fees don't roll in as fast as you expected? That's the advice Kevin Eichner, president and CEO of Enterprise Bank, gave entrepreneurial dreamers when he was a management consultant and they wanted his counsel.

"You might not make any money for a year," he'd say, "and your worst enemy is fear. If you have that reserve, you'll be covered during the rocky early days. Your next enemy is fooling yourself into thinking that activities on stuff like furniture, office supplies, etc. are actually advancing your business. It's critical that you get on the fastest path to cash."

Newbies all head confidently forward, blithely ignoring the battle-scarred entrepreneurs telling them, "It'll take three to five years before you make any money." They learn bitter lessons when the vets turn out to be right. Get that cushion BEFORE you start. You'll have your peace of mind, confidence, and your family's emotional support if you've got the gamble covered.

5. Can you tolerate a 24-hour-a-day job? People sometimes start businesses so they can work fewer hours, then learn they can never leave their job. A client once told me about her parents' being in business together. "At the dinner table," she said, "I felt like we had another child in the family. . .the business."

This is the only question that doesn't demand a resounding, "Yes!" from you. Women run writing or research businesses from home. Crafters bored with mundane weekday jobs work weekend craft shows. An enthusiastic amateur chef starts a part-time catering business to distract him from his IT job. Yes, these are businesses. No, they're not "burn-the-boats" ventures, where the family looks for its major sustenance (and benefits package). That usually comes from somebody's day job.

6. What's your ability to market you and the product? You put yourself on the line each time you pick up that phone. Can you take rejection and keep at it? If you can't, you won't survive long.

Will you succeed? Here are the paths of successful entrepreneurs: (a) You buy (or take over from a family member) an ongoing business and you've worked there a number of years, and you have the courage and drive to be president/owner. (b) You get downsized with a big severance package, which gives you the financial float. (c) You have partners—equally committed —prepared for the hunkering down period and with access to money beyond the house and the credit cards. (d) You had the thousands (or millions) to buy a franchise whose organizational support gives you confidence to proceed. (e) This is your only option. (f) Your spouse (with benefits) sees your employment and income as adjunct. (g) Your dream outshouts and your drive outruns every objection, and your only fit is at the top of the heap.

Try it if you have the savings, the support and the drive. It'll be great experience, if you don't bankrupt the family. Even if you roll back into the corporation, you'll have learned a lot.

Another strategy: Keep a weather eye open for job opportunities. Clients have printed up a consultant's card and gotten business that turned into a full-time job.

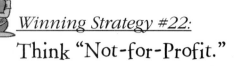

Winning Strategy #22:
Think "Not-for-Profit."

Not-for-profits (NFP) hold an appeal at various career points. One might be at your beginning. You want to make a difference, you have a mission. As one wag put it, you want to "help the needy, not feed the greedy." Another is at mid-career, when the race you've run is either done or grinding you and it feels like time to give back. Another is when you watch the shenanigans of businesses caught in the "bad-boy" spotlight and long for a kinder, gentler workplace.

You should know that the do-gooder organizations may not have the clear distinction you want. They are businesses like any other, and the emphasis is on money. "Profitability" drives the for-profit, "fund-raising" drives the NFP and public/private dollars are increasingly hard to come by. Where once the tiny agency ran on the passion of its founder, today it wants business skills and strategic plans. Meetings are equally endless. NFPs are subject to downturns and layoffs and uncomfortable external investigations just as in the for-profit world. Board members in NFPs tend to be more concerned about operational details, but your access to them (unless you're the executive director) is probably as impossible as at any large firm.

The people may be just as venal in the community clinic as at the giant corporate hospital. William V. Miller, M.D., former lifelong executive of large not-for-profit organizations (and now an executive coach), says, "At not-for-profits, the expectations of altruistic behavior often far exceed the way the organization behaves." In other words, you might find just as many dogs-eating-dogs where your passion for service gets carried out.

How might they be different? Deborah Patterson, president of the Monsanto Fund, says, "You're doing something for the betterment of mankind, to change the world, to make a difference. Not-for-profits, because they're usually smaller, are easier to navigate. You're closer to decision-makers and it's easier to figure out processes and accountabilities. In large corporations, there are more people, more checking. It's not always clear who's responsible for what."

As a business consultant working both sides of the profitability street, I've felt one big difference as I've rambled the halls. NFPs have a mission, it matters TO THE CORE of its people, and—unless the BUSINESS of making the institution run gets in the way —it has an inspiring ongoing effect on employees. They're in it for the higher good.

Are your skills transferable? While friendly doors frequently swing open to the business-experienced, the NFP may not gasp with delight at the prospect of having you. Regulations, systems, ways of doing business can be fundamentally different. Yes, they can be learned, but seekers often have a more optimistic opinion of how quickly it can be done than proves true later. You will be attractive to NFPs if you have a skill they don't have in-house and badly need. Do they need your influence, your customer base, your reputation?

As with any potential employer, learn before you go to the not-for-profit. What is its mission and how do you relate to it? What are the struggles and goals? How well run is it? What do you bring that they need but don't have?

Your desire to serve is commendable and will be appreciated. But the fit also has to be here.

How do I network?

Winning Strategy #23:

Get a P.I.E. or a Target.

Daniel Porot—author, helper of thousands of job seekers, fine human being—has a way to organize your networking. Read his book, *The P.I.E. Method for Career Success* for the full explanation. Briefly, it's a way of beginning your search with broad brush strokes, and narrowing to a job interview.

At the first stage, when you're confused, Daniel says you should seek out meetings for PLEASURE (the "P"). Choose several fields or industries based on your interests. Use them to move from general feelings to focused campaign to the job and title you want in a specific company. He considers the Yellow Pages a great place to start. A particular job sounds interesting to you? Who knows someone? It's remarkably easy, he claims, to find a person and get an appointment. (I agree. In our virtual worlds, who ever asks us about ourselves or what we do all day? We're happy when someone wants to know.)

What do you say when you get there? You follow the same format each time. Daniel calls it: "How-plus-minus-cloud-star-hophophop." These are the questions:

How—How did you get your job?

Plus-minus—What are the plusses and minuses of a job like yours?

Cloud—What are the tasks a person in your job has to perform?

Star—What skills are needed in this job?

Hophophop—Do you know someone else I can talk to about this field? (AND get three names, addresses and phone numbers.)

Follow your interests. If it sounds perfectly awful to run a social service agency, stop seeing executive directors. If a plant production manager's job fascinates you, find others. You will quickly eliminate THIS, but continue to be fascinated by THAT. Find more of THAT. Your objective is to gain knowledge about a field, to learn its language and processes, as well as its requirements. You want to sound like someone who knows.

When you find the job and title that sounds like you, you try the second stage of the P.I.E. method—INFORMATIONAL interviews with people a bit closer to the job that fascinates you. These are more selective, the risk is higher, so you need to be on your toes. These people can lead you to the opening you want. Don't seek out people who actually have the job and would supervise you, or the human resource manager. Hold them for the next stage. Pick the people "next door" to them, who know the function and/or the individual well, someone who can make you more knowledgeable.

Dick Knowdell, teacher of career professionals, cautions against calling it an "informational" interview because some will interpret this as a veiled request for a job interview. He's right, if you're going after those who get asked a LOT (HR managers, high-profile managers with this month's hot jobs.) They will block you. But if you've been handed to the contact by that person's friend/colleague, they'll open their appointment book.

Now that you have all the information you want, go for the third phase, the EMPLOYMENT interview. Here's where you want the supervisor, the HR department, the company president. You know what to talk about, how to look and sound, and you'll come across as skilled the ideal candidate for the job!

Daniel's technique is terrific, but here's another way of looking at this information seeking process: the target approach. You may already have the names of decision-makers who can place you in a job (they're the center of the target). Never go there first. You will be unsure and hesitant, and if you go to the heart of the target and blow it, you've wasted a golden contact. Always start at the perimeter of the target: someone knowledgeable in a related field, teachers of these professionals, the NO RISK interviews. As you proceed, talk with people closer and closer to your target, such that by the time you get there, you'll have the patter and the lingo and the need down. You'll look like a sure thing.

Daniel is a master P.I.E. maker. Let him help you get your piece of it.

Organize a networking strategy, set a target, but start at the edge and work towards the bulls-eye.

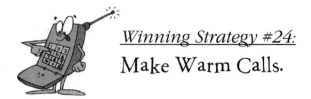

Winning Strategy #24:
Make Warm Calls.

Ah, there's nothing like having your own business! Your business cards look great, your name gleams on the door, and you are ready for customers to burst through, panting for your services.

You discover early that's a fond and fruitless dream. One of your biggest tasks for at least the first two years is to go out and track down the prey, whomp it on the head and drag it back to the cave. In the parlance of business getters, it's called "smiling and dialing." You have a list, and you awaken each day with a firm resolve to make at least 10 cold calls today, telling strangers why they must meet you and your product.

Cold calling can be a deal-breaker for the new and sweating entrepreneur. No, they didn't get your brochure. No, they don't believe they need your service. And—even if you get the appointment—no, that's not what they wanted. If you can't market, you can't be in business.

From time to time, even the best of us punt the "S & D." Our shaking hands just WON'T pick up that receiver, so we make "warm calls," people we know who might be at least somewhat related to what we do, and maybe (please oh please) will do business with us or (phew!) will hand us over to someone in their handheld's address book. The combination of cold and warm calling proves to be good for us and the health of our business.

You're in the same boat as an entrepreneur, pal. During the job search you are in business for yourself, and you have to keep those outgoing lines humming. You learn that warm calls to people you know in positions to help can produce better results faster than the sourpuss to whom you're merely a bother. Here's how to make them:

1. Know what you want to be; don't ask your friend to guess.

2. Say what you want of the friend...a phone number, a lunch, a recommendation.

3. Once you get a contact, call as soon as the friend gives you the go-ahead so you're fresh in the target's mind.

4. Afterwards, call your friend and say "Thanks," or send a note.

5. A note may also be appropriate to the person you called.

6. If the target gave you another contact, make it while it's hot. Leads like this get cold fast.

Curiously, even though warm calls are better than cold ones, you should be making both. This has a synergistic effect. Done together, they work more powerfully. If you leave off cold calling, the warm call results droop. The cold calls are a kind of bracing measure of your cowardice. Like eating your spinach and getting that root canal, this never gets easier, but it vastly improves your life.

When you make cold calls, think first of how the person might benefit from knowing you. Strangers, especially if they're busy and are regularly hounded by others, don't care about you. But if you have something they NEED, viva la difference! Come in! Warm yourself by the fire! So, state who you are, what you want and what might be the benefit to the other of a meeting. You won't hit 100 percent, but enough times to be worth it.

 Tie your red *feng shui* ribbon to the phone cord (it's for prosperity and good fortune), dial up your contact program and get busy on those warm calls and work your way to the cold ones.

Winning Strategy #25:
Walk Through the Door.

S he was graduating in June and wanted to move to St. Louis. She had gotten my name from the Internet, and knew that I did career coaching by phone.

Could I help her get work here? We scheduled a tele-appointment. Her student work background had impressed me; so did her gutsiness and creativity in finding a job in a new city. Coincidentally, right after her call came one from a friend wanting to hire people in the student's field! Could I refer this client to her, I asked. "Absolutely!"

Wow, I thought. Guts and luck. You can't go wrong with that combination. This one will do well. Unfortunately, she didn't keep the appointment or respond to my follow-up phone call.

It reminded me of another woman who sounded determined to get out of her desperate situation. The world often makes way for people like her. Sure enough, an unexpected benefactor heard about her, admired her spunk and offered to help. She never showed up for her appointment with him either.

A third example. Because I know the value of networking, I did an experiment in which I referred ten job seekers to ten people who had agreed to help and who were standing at the doors of opportunity the seekers wanted. When I followed up with the contacts to see how the meetings had gone, I learned that not ONE of the job seekers had even called, let alone walked through the door!

I understand the fears you have about looking for a job. I also understand how difficult the task seems and how hard it is to ask others for help. But I also know how the world often makes way for those who shove open the door of opportunity.

If you are looking for a job, you can make things happen by asking the question, requesting the meeting, setting up the appointment. I know the fear of following through. What if the perfect job ISN'T here? What if you don't impress the person behind the desk? That's why it's easy to blow off the proffered helping hand. But you'll never go anywhere if you let fear scare you away.

 It is remarkably easy to get people to bring you to the door of opportunity. But you have to not only kick it open, you have to walk through it.

Winning Strategy #26:
Take the Train to Chicago.

When I was completing my Coro fellowship (it's a nine-month leadership training program), I decided the time had come to network with other fellow graduates. One of them was the late TV movie critic Gene Siskel. He was with the *Chicago Tribune.*

I wanted to be a writer and he was one. I had several good non-writing job offers and one bad writing one—to be a "stringer" (occasional writer) for a local newspaper. I would attend meetings of the planning commission, municipalities' board meetings, court hearings and I would write about them—assuming I could avoid becoming comatose over my reporter's notebook—and they would pay me the princely sum of $15 per story.

Was THIS the path to writing greatness? What should I do? I called Gene Siskel. I told him I would be in Chicago on a particular date on business, and asked if he would meet with me.

That was a big old lie. I was only going to Chicago if it meant I could meet Gene Siskel. If that didn't work, I would've found out where he went for a drink after work and gone there, or gotten a job as a waitress at the restaurant, or done anything short of stalking to get a minute with him. I also wondered if my networking technique would work, that Mr. Siskel would hand me on to someone else and maybe that would lead to a writing job.

What I got was ten minutes of his time on a park bench outside the Tribune's offices and no referral. He was kind, brisk and firm, and my "lookin' good" slid right off his lanky frame: "I don't think you're a writer, Rose. Writers HAVE to write, and that doesn't seem to be the case with you. Good luck."

What he said to me didn't matter. It was what I took for myself from it. Shuddering at the thought of future Tuesday and Thursday nights parked on the folding chair of a town hall in the west end of nothin', I decided Siskel was right, I should give up that pesky writing notion and take the cushy corporate job being dangled before me.

If you "tsk tsk" about a writer discouraging a would-be writer, you miss the point. I didn't hear what I wanted to hear, but I got what I wanted, some time with a person of influence who I thought might help me. His negative message mattered only in that it helped me make my decision. I decided I wasn't a writer AT THAT MOMENT. That train trip moved me off dead center relative to my career. It got me going in a direction at last.

You also need to "take the train to Chicago," whatever that is for you. Think of someone you might talk to about your career issues. If it makes you nervous to dial the phone, so what? Just say whatever it takes to get the interview. Be where they need you to be when they need you. The $35 that train ticket to Chicago took a significant chunk out of this graduate student's resources, but it was worth every cent.

Winning Strategy #27:
Don't Call Me.

N etworking is the way you'd better live your life, for your soul's health AND to ensure you won't get a crisp, cool response when you're in need.

I'd worked with a guy in the same company. We hadn't seen each other for ten years. He called with "downsized" on his back and "network call" in his voice. I gave him several leads, then never heard from him after he took his new job. Five years later he called again. He wanted to leave this job, and could I give him leads? Hmm. I'd heard from him twice in ten years, both times with his hand out. The milk of human kindness ordinarily gushes in my veins, but this boy's a sap if thinks of this as effective networking or that I was willing to act as if we had a relationship.

THIS is effective networking:

1. Start before you need it. Get out of your desk chair and your tiny world and go be with people. Serve on a board. Ladle out soup in a homeless shelter. Run for the cure of something. Clip an article you saw that a friend might appreciate.

2. Engage with the world. Volunteer if it feels like the right thing to do (but don't say "yes" so much you overwhelm your paid-job time).

3. Develop relationships. A natural outcome will be new friends, reasons to have coffee, numbers to call when you want to see a movie. You'll give and you'll take and you'll bond. Make sure you help others.

4. Rely on it when you need it. If you've LIVED networking, if you've been there for others (and please don't keep score), they'll be there for you. They became friends in soup kitchens and ticket lines and gyms. This is a rich network.

Networking will take you to the resource person who's happy to help, to give you that favor you need, maybe even the direct line to your next job. But it never works when you take a one-sided, desperate approach. Don't wait till you have a pink slip in your hand, your heart in your throat and "Now what?" on your face. If you only exercise your address book when you're in need, I promise you you'll hear clipped, general suggestions on the other end, if your call is even taken.

Don't use people. Make networking a part of your life, and you'll have the lifeline when you need it.

Winning Strategy #28:
Keep It.

The job search process can make us feel as if we've tossed our resume on the altar of some fickle gods who will get back to us when they darn well please, and we have to camp out in front of them till the responding mood strikes them. We quake on our little knees after depositing our cream-colored life story before them. We hunker down and wait…and wait…and wait. After a bit we turn huffy. THEY haven't gotten back to us. THEY'VE kept us in suspense. THEY are bad guys.

From the first phone call or postage stamp all the way to the new employee orientation, YOU have to keep the responsibility for the progress of your search. If the networking contact doesn't return the call, YOU place another one a few days later. Don't be a cyber-stalker though if the person doesn't answer your emails. If you don't hear back after a couple of weeks, call the person who referred you and ask, "What's the deal? I'm not hearing back from Joe." You may have to think of another way in (if the contact is critical to you getting the job you want), or give up on this particular person (if it was for a casual conversation). Only marshal major energy behind major battle lines.

If the personnel office doesn't call after you send in the application, YOU call to learn its status, whether you're a candidate, and when it's appropriate for you to check back. During the interview, YOU find out how long they expect to keep looking, when you'll hear something and what the decision-making process is. Afterwards, YOU call them if you haven't heard anything. When will they make the decision? Are you still in the running? When can you check back?

None of these questions are easy to ask. You don't want to hear bad news, that you're on the list for a "ding" letter, for instance. But it's better to get bad news quicker so you can take back your hopes for THIS job and get going on another. The truth is, recruiters and human resource departments are often overwhelmed with applicants; some don't even have a policy of getting back to applicants. Don't let their delays stop you or make a victim of you or a bad guy of them.

YOU keep the responsibility to keep the flow and the communication and the action going.

What if I still don't have a vision
of what I want to be when I grow up?

Winning Strategy #29:
Do the Career Two-Step.

Y ou face a huge new, complex project whose direction or desired result is unclear. You look at the task, feel shivers of anxiety crawl coldly up your back, and walk away from it. Fear of the big job is the father of procrastination. If the job's too confusing or scary, you'll put it off till the deadline's menacing growl has reached your ears. THEN you get the impossible done.

Planning your career produces that same clamminess. We barely know what to order for lunch. How can we possibly envision our entire working life? If your career path disappears into an impenetrable gloom a few feet ahead of you no matter what you do, look at it another way. Stop trying to get a whole-life vision. Even big companies can't plan effectively beyond three or four years; why should you be any better at long range planning?

Do what the big guys have begun to do. Shorten your vision. Do the career two-step. If you've spent months squinting at your future and haven't blown away the career fog, then narrow your focus to only the next job and the one after that. Ask yourself:

1. What would I like to do next (What seems to be before me now?) and,

2. What job or opportunity might it lead me to?

If you know what you want or CAN do now, you've made the career search bite-size, a problem you know how to solve. If you can say, even vaguely, where you might go after that (and most of us can), then you know how to make the most of the FIRST step, i.e., what to get done while you're in the first job.

Unexpected inspiration could come to you along the way, but doing the "Career Two-Step" is the cure for career procrastination. Just like other impossible projects you've faced, they all had one or two small tasks you COULD do. If you do the smaller pieces, the larger task becomes more doable.

You may never get the view of your Elysian Heights, but you can have a rewarding work life if you learn the "Career Two-Step."

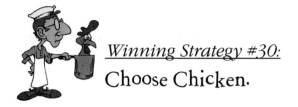

Winning Strategy #30:
Choose Chicken.

Y ou have explored every way around it, but no matter how you heave your shoulder against it, the obstacle remains huge and unbudgable. You look at what stands between you and a career dream. You know others might make a different decision, but you just can't do it. You have an aging parent; you have to pay for kids' college; the economy is treacherously bad; you need the benefits; you can't move to another city. You can't leave or change. Now, what?

Choose chicken. A colleague had made chicken for his children's dinner. They didn't want it. He told them, "Chicken is your current reality. You might as well choose chicken." His point was that, "Here we are, with no alternative. (Pretend there are no Plan B Cheerios and graham crackers in the pantry.) Why make yourself miserable over what ISN'T? Look instead for ways to make yourself happy within what IS. Choose the chicken."

So, too, with you. We all come to a point where we have to live with what IS, like a less-than-perfect job or the "safe" school. You could easily become bitter over the missed chance, the sacrifice. Don't. And don't whine or throw a pity party for yourself, or cast your "guilt" hook into the flesh of the people you did this for.

You CHOSE this. Be a grownup and behave like a chooser. Embrace the decision. You couldn't make any other. Give yourself credit for doing what feels like the right thing. Make yourself happy in place so the decision is more palatable. Look for ways to make the job more interesting. Take a class in your subject.

Find ways to be more valuable. Avoid toxic people. Work on renewing yourself.

BUT KEEP AT THE DREAM. Maybe you can't sell real estate, but you CAN read books and join an association. You can't go to law school, but you CAN take business law classes. You can't try out for the Met this year, but you CAN find the best vocal coach and give recitals in your city. Don't give up what you want to be. There are few times when doors permanently shut, except that I'm thinking of giving up the ballerina dream. Your situation could change but you'll be happier in place and more ready to step into the dream if you've continued to work at your vision.

 You've had to make a tough choice. Congratulations for taking the high road. Just don't turn into a turkey over it. Choose the decision you've made. Choose chicken.

CHAPTER
3

Get the Job

This chapter tells you how to GET the job you want. If you're just moving from one job to another, start here. If you need greater self-understanding or to sound stronger when you talk about yourself in the interview, wander around in the previous chapter.

"Tell me about yourself." "What are your strengths and weaknesses?" "Where would you like to be in five years?" Groan. Interviews put you on the spot, pick at the past you want buried, force you to describe yourself in risky ways. How do you look like what they want while remaining true to self?

The "Cool Career Books" section lists books on interviewing, but the best way to improve your skills is to practice, out loud, in front of somebody who'll tell you where you shine and where you stink. You COULD talk into an audio tape or sit in front of a video camera, but if you don't know what "good" looks like in the interviewee chair, how will you assess yourself? Besides, unless you have more courage than the average bear, you'll clap your hands in horror over your mouth when you see yourself on camera. We all do. Drag someone else into your project.

The thing to remember is to be specific about what job you want, to be who you are in the interview while BEING what they're seeking, to make sure this is right place for you, and to say "Thanks" afterward.

How can I stand out from the rest?

Winning Strategy #31:

Lie on Your Resume. . .NOT!

You want a job, but you have potholes on your career path that could cost you. Can you lie on your resume?

The correct answer, of course, is "Absolutely not." Ethics are important; you want to be viewed as honest, and your resume begins your relationship with a company. Besides, if they catch you lying about education, skills, salary, or experience, you're out the door. You sign your understanding of that on the job application. Lies can cost you plenty. Bob Rosner, author of *The Boss's Survival Guide*, says they're "like time bombs—almost certain to blow up in your face."

The world and its people operate, I find, different from the platitudes we primly espouse. In a recent Internet survey, 8 percent of the respondents said they told blatant lies. Another 27 percent said they fudged and 30 percent made themselves look better than their facts. That leaves about a third of us as squeaky-clean operators.

I am not touting dishonesty, but here are some acceptable ways you can ENHANCE you. Just be careful. If you LIE on your resume you could face joblessness again!

1. You can leave out the job you had for a month or two because it was wrong for you or the company folded. Blips like this make a resume reader nervous. If you have a lot of blips, you have bigger career problems than your resume and you won't make it through the interview. The application demands the whole truth, but by this time your foot is in the door. You've impressed and explained.

You'd better talk about true experience gaps, probably in your cover letter. Time out for kids. Downsized in a buyer's market. Travel in Europe. You don't want to leave questions in the reader's mind. Say what you did and what you got out of it.

2. You don't have to say you were fired. That's the employer's responsibility to discover in the interview, when you SHOULD talk about what happened and why, and what you learned from it.

3. You can upgrade the title you had in the company 10 years ago if that title has also changed. For example, the account manager's job is now called Vice President. That's part of industry's title inflation.

4. You can describe yourself in glowing terms, even if you think you're not as cool as your PR. You need to look good so employers want to meet you. They forgive the pastel overstatement but not neon falsehood.

Sometimes you MUST tell the whole truth. If you're going for a government or other job where someone will closely investigate your background, tell all. If employers uncover information you left out, they won't hire you. Tell your truth, however painful it may be.

When companies rush to fill positions they can neglect to check work histories. If they get flamed, they get cautious and then they check resume facts. When jobs are scarce, they have time. The checker could be your potential boss, the personnel office secretary, a recruiter, or a company specializing in background checks.

A prior employer is only SUPPOSED to release your employment dates, your position and salary; and most companies adhere to it...unless they get the information somewhere else: another friend in that company or a colleague who owes them a favor. They can get it if they want it.

Resume readers know that people puff up their accomplishments. After the first thousand, the puffery becomes obvious. They can tell if you or someone else wrote it and the probable extent to which you tarnished the truth. If it's too much, you won't get considered.

You do have some wiggle room on your resume, but tell the basic truth about yourself. Lie on your resume? I don't THINK so!

Winning Strategy #32:
Tell Me a Story.

You have spent countless hours and possibly money creating your resume. For all its crisp brevity, you might not have created a winning document. You have all the right sections, but may not yet have the compelling story you need to tell. You're not far off, but you're off in the heartbreaking way a world-class athlete barely misses the bronze medal. Only a hundredth of a second separates her from the placeholder, but she's in the stands, not the record book.

Here's how you tell your good story:

1. Know what your industry wants and use that structure. Buy books, software or time with a resume writer to get it right.

2. Tell me a story. We may be eons from our ancestral campfires, but nothing makes a group scrape chairs closer than when someone says, "Let me tell you a story." A great story has simple language, a logical plot and pieces that fit. Its characters travel interesting, tragic, funny or unique paths.

Put a "story" template over your resume and look at it through the eyes of a stranger. Are you a creaking automaton marching toward the corporate maw, or a three-dimensional strider over life's hills? Begin SAYING your story. Jot down what seems meaningful, the American Legion Award in elementary school, the athletic scholarship, your after- school job at the stock brokerage firm. Talk about your post-school jobs. What did the companies do? What were your responsibilities? What are you proud of achieving? Don't forget being a RA in college, Little League coach, treasurer of a board. When you've finished you'll have a rich story to tell on a resume. You may not include all of it, but the reader will understand your journey.

3. Tell me a clear story. Use the language of where you want to go and drop the language of where you've been. Whether finance, auto manufacturing or hotel management, cultures uniquely communicate. Outsiders don't understand the verbiage, so unless you're going from one financier's cubicle to another, use clear, simple words.

4. Tell me the whole story. Your reader must be able to track your work life. If you're in college, include all the ways you scrambled to make money since age 16. If you're at mid-career with many stories to tell, drop the lawns and burger-slinging and focus most on the last 10 to 15 years. DON'T simply list the relevant or good jobs. An interview comes after the resume, and it requests your complete chronology. If your resume has just your high points, the interviewer will doubt your honesty and won't call you back.

5. Tell someone else your story. Show your resume to colleagues or people in the field you're targeting. Ask, "Am I clear? Do I look desirable for the job I want? Have I left out anything?"

 You are fascinating in more ways than you know. Make sure your "resume story" shows that.

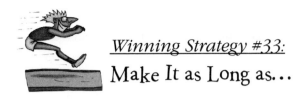

Winning Strategy #33:

Make It as Long as...

W hen you were in school, your career officer told you a lie, or a truth that became a lie. Your burning question then was, "How long should my resume be?" Someone told fresh-faced, no-experienced little you, "One page only!" Who needs more to present the baby-sitter, burger-flipper, Scout, intramural track star you were? Those experiences counted. Hiring managers saw you as responsible, work-minded, mature. How hard it was to fill one page!

Years later, your resume type gets smaller and the margins narrower, as you fit your bigger life into that same small space. "Where did that awful myth originate?" I asked myself, dragging out Coke-bottle-bottomed glasses to read tiny print. "Probably in a placement office without file drawers," I decided.

Dick Knowdell, president of Career Research & Testing, says you should be succinct because, "Employers spend 8 to 10 seconds reading a resume. You'd better tell your career story fast."

Your resume should be as long as is appropriate for your life, industry and geography. Resume writers say the West Coast uses one page; but the East Coast, two pages. Put key-word summaries at the top so computer scanners won't drop you into the cyber-wastebasket.

Want a job with the federal government? Resumes should be three to five pages, and use the government's format.

"Companies in general expect one or two pages," says Kristen Koppen, principal of Koppen and Associates, a recruiting firm.

"Universities, the sciences and medical institutions expect six pages or more. If you're thinking international, resumes are four pages, and different countries have different formats. Some information considered essential on resumes in the U.S. is considered bad manners abroad."

Create a succinct, clear and correct picture of you. Think of your resume like the seat of your jeans. It expands as you get older.

How do I get to the right person?

 *Winning Strategy #34:*
Go Through Big Dog.

You can increase your chance of a response to your resume if it arrives with a return postcard OR carries "Big Dog's" name in the cover letter.

A new client, president of a mid-sized company, was outraged. He'd sent out 125 resumes to *Wall Street Journal*-type firms and gotten only one reply. He knew he had played out his want-ad strategy, but didn't know where to turn. "How rude," he said, "not to get back to me."

You don't get a response because the Internet's push-button, resume-flinging capability can instantly send thousands of resumes. Also, it's not a business convention to answer, so overwhelmed recruiting offices don't. When I was a recruiting manager at a large corporation, my staff plopped only the best-fitting fish on my desk, sending a neutral rejection to the smaller fry. Your resume is an important document to you. Don't make it junk mail. Use it as a targeted marketing piece, not a blanket to cover the job world.

You MIGHT hear from a company 10% of the time if you attach a prepaid, self-addressed and stamped postcard to your cover letter. On its reverse, write a note, asking HR to check as appropriate, and return the card:

__ Not for us. Thanks.

__ We'll get back to you by_____(date).

Name: _____

For _____ (company)

Keep records and follow up two or three weeks afterwards.

The second strategy works far better, as my president client learned when he at last asked Big Dog friends to refer him in to other Big Dogs at various companies. "Use my name," they told him. He got responses because his cover letter's first sentence said, "I am writing to you at the recommendation of Mr/Ms Bigdog." Whenever Big Dog in my company sent a note asking me to consider a resume, I sat up and said, "Woof." I handled the applicant promptly, even walked the resume through the company, often did a courtesy interview. You do not mess with B.D.

Others could also persuade special treatment for applicants. Good Friend, Someone-I-Owed-A-Million-Favors, Someone-I-Wanted-Something-From, or Someone-on-Whose-Radar-I-Wanted-to-Be-A-Darling-Blip. If their names made the first paragraph of the letter, I acted. Ask friends and colleagues to let you use their names; they will, if they love you, or owe you, or they just know this is how business gets done.

 Get to the decision-maker any way you can and you won't pine away waiting by the mailbox. Keep your search campaign in motion.

How do I get past stumbling blocks to the interview?

 Winning Strategy #35:
Do the Overqualified Strut.

Your hi-liter poises tentatively over the Sunday want-ad. "I can do THAT," you say, then with a reluctant sigh, "again." THAT was your job years ago. You grew beyond it, so you're 'way overqualified today; but the wolf growls hungrily at your door and no other jobs peek temptingly from the newsprint. Should you apply?

Hiring managers get squiggly with overqualified candidates. They believe:

1. You'll cost more than they've budgeted, and cheaper help is readily found.

2. If you take a lower paying job, you'll fly the moment the job squeeze eases.

3. You'll be miserable in a job you'll see as beneath you.

Employers follow a logic in hiring. If the job requires horsepower of 20 and you have 280, your excess capacity will only scare them away, not impress them.

"Overqualified" sometimes get hired, though:

1. You went through a massive layoff, the whole industry left town, and you're 55 (the employer knows you're not leavin').

2. This job realizes a long-denied dream. They see how you've trained/prepared the last couple of years, and you've persuaded them a lower income will work for you.

3. Your capabilities are scarce and they can see a bigger slot for you later.

Smaller companies have more flexibility and will take greater risks than a large one. You must network to get in, however. Your impressive resume too handily merits a heave-ho from the receptionist, but a pal inside might get you to the president. You must have knowledge, information or skills that will make dollar-signs dance in their eyes. If they can make money from you AND know you won't bolt, you could have a new career berth.

A desperate 60-year-old came to see me. He'd just been down-sized from his director-level government job. Where would HE find a job?

"Who needs you?" I asked him. "You know all the players and the complications of the government's business. Who needs that intelligence?"

He snapped his fingers, having remembered the ambitious young vendor who'd been nipping at his heels for business. They met and that day he became Vice President of Contracts, a job he happily held for five years.

 "Overqualified" is a hard sell. Hitch up your britches and get creative, need-sensitive, determined, and patient.

Winning Strategy #36:

Pay Attention to Hunting Season.

July and August, November and December feel like awful times to prowl the employment underbrush. "No one will see me," you think. Everyone's either on summer vacation or jigging at holiday parties. Not so. These are the hardest months to motivate yourself, but the best time to be looking.

January and September are the two biggest hiring months of the year. In November/December and July/August, recruiters dial, human resource managers ask employees for referrals, and hiring managers squeeze interviews into vacation or jigging schedules. This underground bustles, and you'll scare up a flapping opportunity if you beat those bushes.

The very QUALITIES of these seasons make people more agreeable about seeing you. Consider the summer. (Who feels like working?) Consider the holidays. (Shouldn't I extend a helping hand to my fellow (wo)man?) You and your request for an informational or job interview, for a networking latté will get kindlier treatment. YOU feel less like working, too, so you'll have to overcome your own lethargy.

The college graduate hunting season is slightly different. The smart guys have had internships and summer jobs to test careers' appeal, from which they may get job offers. If not, their hunt begins by Thanksgiving; interviews in February; and offers start coming in April.

Less-smart guys have a regrettable hunting season that begins after graduation, having made the most of senior year, or stayed too busy completing independent projects. They relax at the rec center pool for a few summer weeks, then dive into the job hunt. Unfortunately, especially if their desired career doesn't have a name, they might have to settle for a mall job for several months. A year as an assistant store manager can create ardent motivation.

It's almost always hunting season. Put on your orange vest and go.

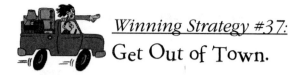

Winning Strategy #37:
Get Out of Town.

Finding work out of town can be difficult. Newly-coined grown-ups can crank up the F-150 pick-up, fill the back with their weights, stereo, PC, blankie and Magic Cards collection, and head off into the sun. Friends at the destination offer a floor for sleeping and help finding wait-staff jobs. They get a ramshackle apartment, then make a serious stab at getting the acting gig, that museum job. *Toujours gaie!*

A few years into the career, the find-a-new-job-out-of-town task is distinctly different. You may be returning to home ground or seeking better opportunities or escaping unfriendly geography. Will the Significant Other relocate? Are there jobs? Do we need nursery schools? What are the 'burbs like? Is there Community for us? Each requirement complicates the choice. And, unless you get lucky, a search can take up to a year.

How do you do get an out-of-town job? The easiest is if a company recruits you and offers to move you - lock, stock and video games - to the new city. Occasionally, such luck happens. Still, it takes time to make the employment rounds, and not all companies will bear the expense of moving you.

Let companies in the desired location know you're available. Monster.com, newspaper ads, recruitment firms. Massage your professional and personal networks as well: association colleagues, friends, your church or college. Go to the library or Web and see what other resources exist. Consider looking up a career counselor in the area who knows the market and can bring your targets into focus. Have a teleconference or two.

See how much effort this can entail?

Travel to Newland, at different times of the year. You may love Arizona's winter but fry like a lizard in summer. Is this the next home for you and your loved ones (and how will you help a teenager who won't leave her friends)? Call it a vacation, but go as a resident. Stay in an apartment. Shop. Find schools and places of worship. Check out the entertainment, sports, outlying areas. How easy is it to get around, make friends, satisfy your passion for sushi? Is there a job seekers club? A special newspaper or web site for people on the hunt like you?

Can you see how this could take a year or more?

You might be impatient, arguing you might as well go. Your "What the heck" attitude has merit. Just take enough money to support yourself for six months while you search. Pay attention to seasonal details like: going in June so the kids have summer to make new friends, or not moving to the mountains in November. A less drastic move is to go by yourself for six months. It's hard on family and pocketbook, but you have a home if the streets of Newtown don't prove to be paved with gold.

Give yourself time and do your due diligence if the horizon beckons you.

How do I get ready for my interview?

Winning Strategy #38:
Hold a Dress Rehearsal.

Opening night at the theater is electric. The actors are excited and nervous, but they're primed. They know their lines. They've gotten through readings, endless rehearsals, including costume and tech, and a dress rehearsal. They know how the costume moves, where the furniture is and what pose to strike at the end of Act 1.

Their dress rehearsal makes their opening night performances dazzling.

As a job seeker you aren't that different from actors. You have lines, stage directions, an audience, and a performance to give. You will be most successful on the day of your interview if you hold a dress rehearsal beforehand. You don't want to fall through an unforeseen trap door or catch your heel on your crinoline or pants leg.

Here's how your rehearsal goes:

1. Get complete information about your interview day, including careful directions, and who will be talking with you. What should you bring or prepare? How long will it last? If you have time, go to the interview site. What's the route? Will unexpected road construction between your house and the company delay you?

Plan to arrive early, so you can experience the personality of the place you might be working.

2. Ask someone to roleplay an interview with you. You think you know your story, but you'll probably stumble if you don't rehearse the chronology of your jobs, a summary of your education, and answers to the tough questions you'd prefer not to answer. Stumbling is not good. Ask for a critique. Practice changes.

3. Try on your interview outfit. Do you look and feel great in it? Sit in a chair in front of a mirror. That's how you'll look to the interviewer. Need to fix or press or switch the outfit?

4. Put everything you'll need in one spot: wallet and money for parking and lunch, directions, a writing folder with pen and paper, a list of questions to ask, copies of your resume/references, your portfolio (if you're an artist or architect), your breath mints.

5. Go to bed early. Do your best to relax and get a good night's sleep. Sleep trick: Focus your eyes on a point across the room high on the wall or ceiling. Your eyes won't like the strain and will try to close. Do this a few times, and you'll be snoozing.

If you do your dress rehearsal, then the next day, when the house lights dim and the curtain rises on your play, "My Interview: A Tale Worth Telling," you'll step to your mark on center stage, a confident star.

Winning Strategy #39:

Don't Pull Your Skirt Down.

This is NOT an invitation to wear "hubba hubba" clothes to the interview; you know, the attractive short skirt that will alluringly creep up your thighs as you squirm to come up with the best answer about your passions for work. Wear clothing to the interview that is NOT provocative or too tight or that will cause you a second's worry or embarrassment. You must be fresh-faced, focused on and alert to the questions, the job and the place. If your outfit distracts you, you can miss important cues or information.

Think of yourself as a talking billboard. Your appearance and your words advertise you as a potential employee. What message are you conveying? Follow these few guidelines and you'll make a positive impression:

1. Dress appropriately for the job, whether it's a polo shirt and chinos for a warehouse job or smart charcoal gray suit for the corporate suite. Make sure it's comfortable; don't experiment with new and unworn. You should know how it behaves as clothing, walking or sitting down.

2. Wear what makes you feel great, and I mean from the skin OUT. What flatters your face? Makes you look sharp or sophisticated? If you feel wonderful, you'll telegraph that through every pore.

3. Wear comfortable, nice shoes that won't torture, no matter how many halls or stairs you have to trudge. It's hard to keep "pinching shoe" pain off the face, harder still to keep up in stilettos.

4. Be impeccable. You don't have to wear expensive (unless it's the Big Time), but it must be clean, fresh and hemmed and in possession of its buttons. Shoes are shined; heels are all there, not scuffed away.

Your clothes are a big part of the story you tell. Make sure it's a good one.

Winning Strategy #40:
Sing.

Don't walk out that door yet. You're not totally equipped for your interview. Make an about-face and head toward your CD/tape collection. Find your favorite tunes, whether by Pacco or Pavarotti. Are you a tenor, a heavy metal dude or a do-wop girl? Pick music you love to sing. Take the tunes to your car (obviously, this doesn't work in the subway), fire them up, close your windows and warble your favorite songs at the top of your lungs all the way to the interview.

Professional singers and speakers always warm up their vocal chords. An interview is also a performance, act like a pro. Hum the songs through your nose and throat for a couple of minutes to warm the chords and expand your range. Then sing, taking deep breaths and pulling your voice from the barrel of your chest (not the back of the throat) so your sound is rich and full. Sing till you get there (or about 20 minutes), but don't take your music into the waiting room. They're fussy about quiet decorum in office buildings.

Interviews are tension-producing events. Vocalizing will relieve some of your tension; you'll feel more confident. You'll yodel more oxygen to the brain; you'll feel and be more alert. You won't worry all the way about making a good impression, so you'll make a better one. Also, your voice will sound better, calmer, richer, more pleasant. The richer voice is a minor point; a more relaxed you is major.

Sing out, so you can carry your tune in the interview.

What will make me shine in the interview?

Winning Strategy #41:
Sell Trees.

A motivational speaker tells the story about a real estate agent mocked by his co-workers for the high price he, in a down market, slapped on a big house on a big lot with 18 trees that marked the property's back border. "I'll sell it," he assured them.

On the first day the first buyer who came exclaimed over the trees. "It looks just like my boyhood home's back yard!" he exclaimed. Hmm. When they went to the dining room, the agent pointed out the view of the trees. In the upstairs bedroom, the agent noted how the trees looked from here. Even though the buyer balked at the price, he bought it that day FOR THE ASKING PRICE.

Agog at his achievement, his fellow agents asked how he'd sold that house. "I didn't sell a house," he replied, "I sold 18 trees."

The agent, in other words, found what was meaningful to the client and never got off the point. He might have been more personally impressed by the fireplace or the updated kitchen or the accent lighting in the front. If these amenities meant nothing to the client, no pitch would make the sale.

You must take this same savvy to an interview. Find out what they need, and then BE that. But BE that in a genuine way. Too often, job applicants become little parrots repeating back the newspaper or Internet ad almost verbatim. "I'm a team player; I have had increasing responsibilities in management; I am eager to get to the top."

Bogus. You make no impression that way. Tell the potential employer what you mean by that. What evidence can you give that you're a team player? What are the specifics of your growth as a manager? How has your career progressed?

In preparing for the interview, look at the company and the job. What in your background suggests you're the right person? Be ready to say precisely HOW. You can say more about yourself than just these points, but let them know you're what they're looking for.

The interviewer may not even have a window in his office; but, believe me, you're there to sell trees.

Winning Strategy #42:
Don't Drool.

You may tell your work history dozens of times during a job pursuit. Be careful to make your life story interesting… to you.

One job could require a half-dozen meetings with employers asking the same tired questions. Or, you could interview for a dozen different positions. In any case, your breathtaking story begins to wilt after its third or fourth telling. You're so bored with it, your eyes glaze over, your head tilts, and drool runs out the side of your mouth.

But if you go on automatic pilot, the interviewer snaps out of her 3:30 slump, thinks, "I GOTTA get a rise out of this wiseacre," and goes hunting for snappier data. You never want to rouse her hunting instinct because she could track down what you wanted hidden. No, you want her head resting on her hand as she bites her tongue to keep awake because the Diet Coke just didn't do it.

It IS hard to roust up high-performing energy, but you must be like a method actor, and dig down to your toes for enthusiasm and excitement. You must say in your perkiest voice, "And in five years I hope to be in management." Yes, you've said that a zillion times (you don't even know if you mean it). But you have to say it as if it's the first.

the Point

As you settle in your interview chair and watch your interrogator shuffle through her papers, I want you to sit up, grab that imaginary mike, put "fresh" on your eager face and snappily reply to that "five-year-career-goal" question.

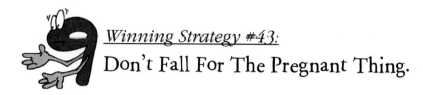

Winning Strategy #43:
Don't Fall For The Pregnant Thing.

You're sitting in the interview. You gave a slick answer to a tricky question, but you thought it sounded pretty good. The interviewer says nothing, just looks at you—warm eyes, warm smile—and your stomach flip-flops. Uh oh. Why isn't she moving on to the next question? Why is she just sitting there, smiling? I can't stand this! You open your anxious mouth.

A minute later, your sweat-drenched body sags against the chair back. You've just told her something you never planned to say about this situation, correctly fearing it would put you in a bad light. Where did THAT True Confession come from?

You just fell for an interviewer's trick that almost always succeeds: the pregnant pause.

Here's how it's taught: When the candidate gives you an answer you think stinks, don't go on to the next question. Sit there expectantly—warm eyes, warm smile—as if you're sure the candidate hasn't finished answering the question. Silently count to "9"—that's why it's called the "pregnant pause." It feels like nine months to the job- seeker. Usually, by the time you get to "5" or "6," the interviewee won't be able to bear the silence, and will blurt out information he'd hoped to keep from you.

the Point

Break the spell of the pregnant pause. When you've finished your response and the interviewer sits waiting and smiling, break eye contact. Look down for a few seconds and breathe. When you look up again, you won't feel as anxious to talk, and the interviewer —now the uncomfortable one—will shift in her chair and move to the next question.

How do I deal with difficult or negative issues?

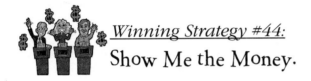

Winning Strategy #44:
Show Me the Money.

(For a great treatment on how to talk dollars, read Jack Chapman's Negotiating Your Salary: How to Make $1000 a Minute. *Do NOT go into salary discussions like a moth heading for a blue bug zapper.)*

If you're a hot commodity in a smokin' field, companies will go to great lengths to hire you, give you perks, signing bonuses and more money than your gape-mouthed parents ever dreamed of making. You have an exciting game to play, and you'd better get smart at it. This strategy is for the rest of us who compete mightily for scarce jobs.

Most companies, large and small, have a range in mind when they go to the market with a position to fill. They seldom change unless they discover to their dismay the price of this particular job has soared, after which they reluctantly ratchet up the salary; OR they realize you bring so much unexpected talent to the company they MUST have you (think of this as rare).

One of your most burning questions is: "What does this job pay?" Seems kinda basic for all concerned. You want something that feels right for YOU; the company wants to attract the appropriate talent. Yet the answer can be as difficult to get as opening up a trick box with a hidden spring. Companies play a "no-tell" game with you. Note to companies: TELL PEOPLE THE SALARY!

Until they figure out what a keen solution that is, there are three times to bring up salary: in your initial contact, in a preliminary phone interview and at the end of the face-to-face.

Because want ads can be confusing, you can't tell the level or salary. If the job seems like one for you, call the company. They'll explain the position. They may not tell you exactly, but you might get the RANGE of salary. If they're too coy for that, ask, "Is it over $50,000 or under?" (or what feels in your range). You need to know if it's worth your time to pursue an interview. Get clever and call your professional association or school or other friends in the field, who can give you relevant information.

Should you give your salary history in responding to an ad? Generally, no. Let them first meet you and love you. Realize, though, that cyber-boards ask for it and won't let you proceed with any blank spaces. Do it.

The phone interview filters the candidates the organization might want to interview. It's generally brief and fact-seeking. One of the questions will be about what salary you want. Push back: What's the range? If the screener won't say and YOU don't respond, you're out. So, give YOUR range. If it's too high, you'll be filtered out, unless scarcity or raw talent keeps you in.

At the formal interview, the salary dance has an etiquette. Hold your questions till the end, as if how you're going to put food in your children's mouth is a tiny afterthought instead of a key point of the exercise. As much as you can, push back with a question. (In other words, you want to get as much as you can, so get what's in their minds before you stamp the sale price on your rump.)

Interviewer: So, what are you looking for in terms of salary?
You: What range did you have in mind?
Interviewer: We wanted to get a sense of what you want.
You: What did the last person make in this position?

Know how companies think. No one sets out to pay the highest dollar. This is business. They want to get the best talent for the least money. They may have little "give," especially if it's a social service agency or small company. They have a range. If you're 'way below it, they worry you don't have the experiential heft for the job. If you're 'way above it, they know you'll scoot when times get better.

Companies who think right want to bring on board a happy camper. Money helps. Being able to pay the chosen candidate a bit more than at the last job also helps. When it can work perfectly, here's how it goes: The range is $50,000 to $60,000. The hottest candidate made $51,000 in his last job. You offer $55,000, which is higher than he made, but it still gives you (the company) room for him to grow in increases. Everyone's happy.

Regarding negotiation give-and-take, you can play extreme hardball anytime you want. Having observed the game hundreds of times, I can tell you you generally have one salary pushback before the company says, "That's a firm offer." They frequently have more flexibility with expense-related items (bonus, perks, reimbursements). Your negotiation must match the company's personality and your position in it and how badly they want you. If it's a "take-no-prisoners" place, get all the ducats. If it's a proper and corporate home, you may hear one firm figure. If you're at the bottom of the totem pole, good luck. As soon as the offer is made, get it in writing.

the Point   Always go for as much as you can, but go smoothly and with savvy so you feel evenly matched at playing the money game.

Winning Strategy #45:
Don't Dodge the Ack-Ack.

You have on your game face. Your toes twinkle as you dance through the interview. Suddenly, the interviewer throws out a show-stopper: Did you ever get fired? Why did you have three jobs in five years? Why is there a two-year gap on your resume? Tell me about a time you failed at something.

You hate those questions. If you tell the bald truth, will you lose your chance at the job? What are they looking for?

We all have little "uh-ohs" in our career basket that we'd prefer to keep tied up and hidden: You left a good job for a promising opportunity, but your boss was a psycho and you bolted six months later. OR: You suffered a depression after getting downsized and didn't really look for work for a year. OR: You got fired because you just didn't do your job. How do you talk about THAT?

Interviewers have good reasons for the questions. One is they're simply trying to get the facts, ma'am. The way you've put your life together gives them a picture of what you'll be like as an employee. Another is they want to see how you respond to unexpected pressure; how you behave when you're as suave as if posing for your corporate photograph—manicured hand on well-toned hip—and the ack-ack guns start. Finally, they want to know how emotionally fit you are. Are you solid enough inside to say, "Yeah, here's who I am, warts and all. I'm not afraid to be what I am."

When you fell down and scraped your high-potential knees, how did you recover? What did you learn from it? All of those reasons add up to how maturely you will behave on the job. IT'S NOT

WHAT HAPPENED TO YOU. IT'S WHAT YOU DID WITH IT.

Know in advance how you'll respond to the ack-ack questions. Before the interview, jot on a piece of paper the things you DON'T want to talk about, the questions you hope you WON'T get asked, and—with the above paragraph in front of you—jot down what your answers would be; and then rehearse them with somebody who loves you, warts and all. The best way to answer the "I screwed up" questions is: This is what happened, this is what I did and this is what I learned from it. The best way to discuss the issues you're not sure about (taking off a year, for example): Say what you did and why you did it and why it did or didn't turn out to be a good decision for you. Concerning the bad boss: This is one time when IT'S ALL ABOUT YOU. Talk about YOURSELF and what you were seeking, not the psycho boss you were fleeing.

Regarding the ack-ack question that comes out of nowhere (and no matter how well you prepare, you'll get one), here's how you deal with it: Break eye contact with the interviewer (it puts you back in your own soul); pause (if you're brave enough to stand the silence), say something that lets you delay a moment, like: "That's an interesting question," or "You're asking if I ever did a project where I wasn't at my best?" You want to get into your own head, maybe reframe the question as I just did, so you give yourself those nanoseconds to prepare your comeback. You don't have to give rapid-fire answers and they don't have to be perfect. In fact, it's a point in the "plus" column if you DO take a THINK pause. Give a straightforward, brief answer, see if you can say something you learned and then SHUT UP.

Don't B.S. your answer. It causes the interviewer to put his nose on your trail to sniff out the truth. Then you REALLY lose because he knows how to track you down and he can fluster the feathers off of you.

Regarding your gray areas—things you aren't great at, getting eased out of the organization—if the interviewer doesn't ask, don't volunteer the information. Don't be the chicken looking for the farmer's wife holding an axe in her hand.

 If you can answer difficult questions with calm and mature honesty, the interviewer will move on. You want him to say, "Isn't that interesting? Now, for the next question."

Winning Strategy #46:

Vacation in the Canaries.

Months ago, looking up from your snow-banked drudgery, you found a bargain vacation on Tenerife. Seeing you could just swing it with your frequent flyer miles, you and the spouse said, "Let's go to the Canary Islands for vacation next July." You sent off many non-refundable dollars to book your share of an island paradise.

Then the job loss thing unexpectedly happened, but you worked hard and got lucky. You've just had a great interview and know they'll make you an offer; but they've set a start date of July 1. What do you do about Tenerife?

You go. Why?

1. Companies always dither about getting the interview process started, but they inevitably want the job winner to start yesterday. Few jobs truly must start NOW.

2. You'll lose your vacation downpayment if you cancel, maybe your spouse as well if you say, "We can't," or "Go on without me."

3. Going through the job-losing and -getting process is hard on a family. You need a break and you won't get a vacation again till next year. Better rest up this summer.

When might you have to forego the beach? When you might, in fact, lose the job over it. It could happen if you and another candidate are considered an even match, or there really is a critical reason for one start date: Start of a school year and the students need you, the teacher, a national meeting at which you'll meet your new area managers to discuss goals for the year; the space shuttle lifts off on July 4 and you're the dispatcher. If you have to lose the vacation, at least ask if the company will reimburse you and/or give you the time to schedule it again or negotiate a refund with the resort.

Should you have laid this all out in the interview? Maybe. Typically, the interchange goes like this:

Interviewer: When are you available to start?

You: August 1.

Interviewer: (Writing) Mmmph.

If you get pushed on the date, put Tenarife on the table. They might let you start in June and get that July time off. If you're high enough in the company, you might not even have to take the time without pay. There is a slight negative cost to your hopping out of the work pond just after you've hopped in. Beginnings are too important to be short-sheeted, but you can make up most of it by working extra before you go and taking some work with you. (Sorry, spouse. We're taking the long view here.)

 Almost all start dates are pushable. Have a good reason for doing so; don't make them wait more than a few weeks for you, and go bury your toes on warm sand.

How can I continue to impress them after the interview?

Winning Strategy #47:
Do What Your Mom Told You.

Christmas, for all its fragrances and good will, had its dark side when you were a kid. No matter how many presents you opened, it was never enough; you wanted more. And, your mom said you couldn't wear it or spend it or play with it till you wrote thank-you notes to your relatives. Life was torture.

"Dear Aunt Jolene," you sighed in your annoyed but obedient scrawl. "Thank you for the $10. I will save it for something useful." (This is your mom's dictate.) "Happy New Year." Bam! In the envelope and out the door for CDs!

Now, all grown up and finished with that interview or networking meeting, imagine your mama is holding out pen and paper and telling you to get busy on thank-you notes...to everyone you met, please.

You can be remembered for your thank-you notes if you'll throw away your dutiful but dull Aunt Jolene model. In fact, asserts career author Daniel Porot, a thank-you note can mean you'll get the job over your competition and tells how a note broke the tie between two candidates the search committee loved.

"You sent a note," the woman was told when asking how they decided on her. "We couldn't make up our minds because you were both so great. Then your note came, and we decided you would go the extra mile on the job, too, and that made our decision."

Here's how to get that competitive edge AND be memorable.

1. Pay attention while you're interviewing! Get the names and cards of people you meet. Notice everyone's environment, things THEY might be interested in.

2. Take notes during your interview. What stands out to you. . .a bonsai tree (and you discover you both love them). . .a photo of the interviewer on the company softball team (and you gabbed about life in right field). . .a striking comment the interviewer made about why she came to work there.

3. As soon as you get home, grab that Mont Blanc or Bic and a nice notecard and get this task done. The truly awesome do it in the car or at a coffee shop before going home! Every day that passes without note completion increases the probability you'll never do it. Being late with this also sends a negatively tinted message about your timeliness. Don't type it or email it or take the content from a book.

4. Adopt a warm, me-to-you, conversational tone. Imagine you're with that person.

5. Do this format as your content: (a) Opening line. You could jump right into the "Thank you for meeting with me," but to be memorable, imagine you're writing a story, and you want something to grab the reader), like:

> *It was so fun talking with you about your trophy-winning home-run last season on the B-Co Bearcats. You gave me hope that the Bronx Blisters can...*

or

> *Most people only dream of going on exciting adventures, but you actually realized yours when you climbed Devil's Tower. An amazing accomplishment.*

Notice that the content is about the receiver of the note, not you. A sure-fire winning beginning. (b) Second line. "Thank you for meeting with me." (c) Next line. Tell the person something memorable or that you learned in your meeting. Make sure it's not an overhead, vague point, but something meaningful.

> *I thought about the steps you described in becoming a global company, and I was impressed to learn how the company built a virtual workforce.*

or

> *You mentioned that the company's challenges lie in reaching the teen-age market, and I agree with you that a method such as Visa Bucks can take you there. Certainly, that was my experience at teeneagle.com.*

Don't make the receiver gag over sugar-y insincerity. Keep the Eddie Haskell phoniness out of it. (d) If you just KNOW you're the person for the job, say you'll send under separate cover your thoughts on (pick what fits): A possible marketing strategy, how you'd tackle the retention problem, how you'd make the warehouse efficient. (e) Last line. "I look forward to working with you. Thanks again." (f) Be contact-able. Under your name (even though this isn't good notecard form), write your phone number and email address so the recipient can easily contact you again.

People have been known to save well-crafted thank-you notes.

If you're not qualified for the job you just interviewed for, a thank-you note won't change the company's mind. But it could improve your chances and make you look like your mama raised you right.

What should I do while I wait for the decision?

Winning Strategy #48:

Keep Looking.

You've just come from a dynamite interview. You were well prepared, in peak form. You answered every question perfectly and watched the interviewers' heads nod approvingly. You loved them and they loved you. You just know you're going to get an offer.

Don't count on it.

You are not necessarily a good judge of what's really going on with a company's job search. They may already have an internal candidate, but Personnel has forced them to do an outside search first. The guy who was the most charming and who loved you the most may be on the political outs in the company and will therefore have a weak voice in the final say. They may just be charming interviewers. You could have read the winds wrong that day. You may be one of TWO candidates they truly love. A less-qualified relative of the president may walk in after you. Game's over.

There are many possibilities, but you have no control over them, so don't waste time worrying. Also, don't use a great job interview as an excuse to stop interviewing. You don't get to quit till you have a job offer in hand that feels like the one you want. Keep looking. Make those contacts, write those letters, follow up on those phone calls and informational interviews. If an offer comes, you won't have made yourself crazy waiting. If someone else gets the offer, you won't have fallen behind in your search.

 **Keep looking.**

What if I don't get the job?

Winning Strategy #49:
Deal with It.

Not every interview turns into a job offer. What do you do if the company rejects you?

What we'd like to do is climb in our crib and wail, or go downtown and give that interviewer a piece of our mind. But we're adult, so we don't do things like that. There we sit, with a painful hole where our stomach used to be, where the cannonball of rejection hit us, while our drill-sergeant spouse or self-appointed cheerleader friend is telling us to get up off our keesters and get going.

I believe, especially if it was a job you particularly wanted, it's important you take a day to be sad about it. Stay in bed with the covers over your head. Be mad or sad, or both. Say all the horrible things you want to say about the company. Draw pictures with black crayon of the boss you might have had, and cut it up into tiny pieces, while cackling gleefully. Mope.

As the day goes on, however, and you've said all the childish "I hate you, I hate you" chants, you gradually return to the grown-up world. Sit with a pencil and paper and go back through the interview. Write down where you think you did well and not so well. Try to see it from the company's vantage point. How do you think they saw you? What did they seem to be looking for?

This is probably no consolation to you, but it's true nonetheless. The fact that you got to the interview meant you had the basic qualifications. It is also true that the person who got the offer may have had a slight edge in qualifications, but it is overwhelmingly probable that the one who got the job was viewed by the company as "a better fit for us." Companies hire someone based on a subjective, almost indefinable something that tells them this is a match. "I like the guy" is the bottom line—even the sole criterion sometimes—for the hiring decision.

You may feel they didn't appreciate you, or that gender/race/age bias was at work, or the person chosen had half your qualifications. True or not, you gain nothing by letting this distract you from your task: Be sad, mine the experience for next-time interviews, and get going again.

Winning Strategy #50:

Learn Where to Improve.

Can you call the company and find out why you didn't get the job? No, and yes. In companies where Human Resources control the hiring process, hiring managers often refer calls to HR, where you will only be told that someone more qualified was hired. End of phone call. The concern is that you might take some action against the company if you decided in the conversation you were more qualified, and you had their words to go by. So, they don't get into the conversation in the first place.

On the other hand, you can often get information if the hiring manager's company has a different HR approach, or if you ask the question in the right way. Never refer to the other guy who got the job. Never ask for comparisons of skills. Red flags will fly through those phone wires, and any sensible manager will tell you nothing.

State that you want to learn from this interview session about how to better prepare yourself for the next one. What should I emphasize as my strengths next time? Where did you see areas where I can grow? Are there ways I could improve my interviewing skills?

You could still get the cold shoulder or the referral to the HR black hole, but you have a better than even chance of finding out why you didn't get the job.

No matter how wrong you think the company was not to hire you, you must be a 100% good sport about it. Send your thank-you letter. Say you're sorry you didn't get the job, and express the hope of being considered for another opening. You may have been the Number Two draft choice; Number One might not finally take the job, and you could be the one they hire, particularly if you're qualified AND a nice guy. If you thought this job truly was for you, and it appears hopeless with the company you just interviewed, then think about approaching its competitors. Maybe they need someone like you.

At the very least, you should have gained self-knowledge that will help you do better and make fewer mistakes in your next interview go-round.

The pain of rejection is just awful, even if you weren't that interested in the position. We want to be wanted. But I've worked with hundreds of people who've had that experience, and in almost every instance, as time went by and other opportunities came along, the person didn't feel lasting regret about not getting the job. Maybe we all have boundless ability to kid ourselves, but the job we didn't get offered turns out in the end not to be the job we truly wanted.

 **Learn, get up, get moving.**

Should I take a job I don't want or that pays too little?

Winning Strategy #51:
Beware of Kidney-shaped Tables.

You've gotten a job offer. It isn't the one you wanted, but you're pretty sure you can make the best of it if you take it. All I can say is: Beware of kidney-shaped tables.

When I was nine, I loved traversing the alleys near my house and dragging home neighbors' discards, the gleam of hope in my eye and the thump of confidence in my heart that I could turn this trash into a treasure. We lived on the wrong side of the wrong side of the tracks, nothing was a treasure to begin with, so you can imagine how trashful it must have been to be pitched. We were poor but proud, and my humiliated father would make me drag it right back, over my protests about its potential.

When I went out on my own, I took my "trash to treasures" idealism straight to the Goodwill Store where I intended to furnish my first apartment. I found a kidney-shaped coffee table. Retro and cool now, then it was embarrassingly out of style. That didn't matter to me. I had transformative plans.

Antiquing was all the rage. You take old furniture, slap on a base coat (mine for this table was black), let it dry; then brush on and wipe off a top coat (mine was royal blue). Voila! New life breathed into the old. When my table was finished I looked at it with dismay. I had imagined this post-modern drek becoming quaint, maybe Victorian, certainly with different lines than it still had. No matter the paint and my effort; it was still an ugly, *outré* kidney-shaped table.

I love my "trash-to-treasures" mentality. Comes in handy when "careers" is your career, and people's potential excites you. But this was an important lesson that something must first have the bones, an essential is-ness, if it's going to be what you want. This is critical to know whether you're giving new life to old furniture, picking a mate, or taking a job. No amount of work on your part will turn 1950s sleek into late Victorian fussy.

When you get a job offer, your first reaction is relief. You can SMELL the end of this awful job search, FEEL the crinkle of a paycheck envelope. You've found a job! But be careful. Is this job right for you, or is it a kidney-shaped table? Think back on the interview. What did you think of the people you'd work with and for? Did you like and respect them? What about the work itself? Interesting and challenging, or boring and beneath you? Will there be more overtime than you want? More travel than your family can tolerate? Do you feel excitement or dread when you think about your first day there?

You may have to run a job offer through a second test: Have I been out of work long enough that I just need a job? We all face that grizzly bear sometimes. If you have to take it, do; but go knowing why, and with the determination to make a switch when you can.

If you have a choice, race right past the job offer that looks like a kidney-shaped table. No amount of spin will make it different than it is: the wrong place for you. It's hard to keep going, but it's not worth it to settle too soon for a job you'll hate. Never settle for trash if treasure lies as a possibility ahead.

Winning Strategy #52:

Hope You're not a Tulip.

You've been on the hunt forever and you've finally landed an offer! You love everything about the job - your team-mates, the boss, the challenges to come, the color of the bathroom - except for one teeny-weeny problem. The salary is teeny-weeny. Should you take a job that pays less than the one before?

Sometimes you can:

1. Your previous job was in a high-paying area of the world, and your skills in this city net much lower offers.

2. You had a terrific run up a fat ladder and it collapsed. Remember the tulip mania in 17th century Holland? The flowers were rare, the wealthy coveted them. Their prices skyrocketed and vast fortunes were made by speculators, called "blommists." Competition became so keen for them, one bulb in 1624 sold for the equivalent of $2,250, plus a horse and carriage! That party ended when tulip trading crashed in 1637. They've kept their affordable status since.

Could you be an expensive tulip bulb in a collapsed flower market? The money's never going to be there, so you have to settle for a lower salary.

3. This new job will provide a unique on-the-job education and you can trade significantly up on the experience a couple of years from now.

4. You're at a different time of your life and you don't need the same level of earnings. If this is your situation, you'll have to

sell the employers on why you'd work for less. They suspect lower competence or "plan to go when times get better" in the candidates willing to take less money.

How MUCH less can you accept? Do this math. You were making $50,000. The new job pays $45,000. Your anticipated increases will range from $500 to $2,000 a year. It'll take several years, in other words, to get back to your current level. If there's a $20,000 difference you won't recover, unless you can quickly leap into bigger jobs.

You are a valuable tulip, no matter what you decide to do. Just be sure you give yourself enough for food and sunshine and regular showers.

CHAPTER 4

Do the Job

You slicked up your resume, breezed through the interviews, and got your references to say glowing things about you. They bought it! You finally scored the job you wanted.

Getting the job is only the first challenge. Keeping it is the rest. You want to make a good impression on others, to make friends, to enjoy the eight or ten hours a day you'll spend at work. You need to learn the ropes as well as the politics. You want to make a good first impression, build relationships, make an impact, get along with the boss, swim well in what can be murky waters. You don't know the rules and there's no lifeguard on duty.

The first day on the job is terrible. All these new faces, a job you don't yet comprehend, people speaking in "culture-ese." Suddenly, everything you hated about your old job seems desirable. Everything in the new place seems exactly wrong. You feel awful, but you know you shouldn't cry on your first day. You will feel better soon, so keep your chin up and move forward.

You need to start off on the right foot and get yourself into the game. Think of this chapter as your life preserver while getting skilled at paddling.

How do I get off to a good start?

Winning Strategy #53:
Be Bright-Eyed and Bushy-Tailed.

You only have one chance to make a good first impression. When we encounter something new, we laser-print the information on our cyborg brains. You CAN rub out a bad first impression, but it takes patience and cyber-sandpaper.

1. Learn all about the first few days so you move confidently through them. Call your contact at the company. Where should you report, and to whom? What will be your schedule? Call your new boss and ask more about responsibilities, projects and goals. If you ask questions you seem smart, not stupid.

2. Look and act your best on the first day. Select clothing appropriate for your workplace. If the environment is Ivy League and you show up as Casual Friday, yikes! Press and polish it to perfection.

3. Get a good night's sleep.

4. Lay out everything you'll need, from your pantyhose to your #2 Ticonderoga pencils. Avoid last-minute emergencies. You have to arrive at the office looking cool and focused and ready.

5. Get there early the first few weeks. Be a bright, perky, friendly part of the team. Stay late.

the Point

You'll seem eager and ambitious, which contributes to that practically unshakable first impression.

Winning Strategy #54:
Move the Flagpole.

Move the flagpole" allegedly comes from military lore. When a commander takes a new post, he moves the flagpole at the front gate. If it had stood to the right of the gate, he moves it to the left. If it was near the guard house, he moves it away. Why? To let everyone know—coming and going, day and night—things are different.

At your new job, look for a flagpole to move, whether or not anyone reports to you. Hang art. Rearrange the desk's orientation to the door. Put a message on the departmental voicemail. Move staff meetings from Friday to Tuesday. Hold meetings with the people you're serving or reporting to. Walk through the plant.

If you like to cook, make seven-layer taco salad for the coffee room. Go to lunch with a new person every day. Become known to others.

Remember the names of the people you meet. (A tip within a tip: When you meet someone, get the other to talk, but don't pay attention to the content. Silently repeat the person's name, while trying to remember something visual about the person. Associate the name and the cue. Bid farewell saying the name. You'll probably remember the name AND the content next time.)

Move the flagpole. Let folks know you intend to make a mark.

Winning Strategy #55:
Get the Right Pencil.

If you want to perform well, all day everyday, you MUST have the right pencil. People with ADD (Attention Deficit Disorder) learn the hard way that performing can be almost impossible without the right tools. Maybe they're hopeless at writing with a pencil, but they do fine with a PC for note-taking. Or, rubber-grip pens help them focus. They struggle all their lives, wondering what's wrong about them—so smart, so unable to learn.

The unafflicted scoff: "Just buckle down!" They believe you can still get things done if the sufferer will make do.

Your organization may "make do" all the time: busted desks, tilting chairs, first generation computers. You might tolerate it because you passionately believe in this underfunded cause. Even so, your work space should be nice and reasonably efficient. If the place needs safer furniture that won't strain your back, speak up. If your cubicle is hot, bring in a fan; or a light if it's dark. Wear headphones if the noise around you distracts. You'll feel and perform better.

We all have idiosyncrasies, odd things about us that appeal for reasons we can't explain. I like writing with soft-leaded mechanical pencils on unlined paper. I work best if I'm listening to a tape of ocean sounds. I get little done unless I make a "to-do" list each day. It sounds goofy; but these tools work for me.

the Point　You spend too much of your life in your work place. Get to know who you are and what you need, and get the "right pencil."

Winning Strategy #56:

Act Like Florrie.

Why not lighten your spirit first thing in the morning, and act like Florrie?

In the A and M, are you a rare bird who pops up from the Sleep of the Innocents, happy with self and world, ready for today's challenges? (We do not like people like this.) Or, do you cling to your headboard, loathe to give up warmth and comfort? Do the claws of yesterday's terrors still cling to you? Do you question your ability to put thumb and forefinger together? Do you hang—boneless and witless—on the edge of your bathroom sink, seriously questioning your ability to brush your teeth up and down and sideways?

Life eventually shines its kindness on us. Like the sun on the spring dew, these grim feelings tend to wisp away as we HAVE to put on a happy face. Whether it's the family, the carpool or the boss, something usually persuades us to drop our grouchiness. The trouble is, you might bite off a few loving heads along the way. Also, you could drag your foul humor with you all day and make everyone miserable.

Florine Mark is head of Weight Watchers' midwest region. She began as a member with weight to lose, got a Weight Watchers franchise when divorce gave her five kids to feed, and she built her organization to its roughly 150,000 members today. Florrie's first task every day is to chase those "Oh, God, it's morning" blues. She stands at her bathroom mirror and talks to herself.

"You're great!" she cheers at her image. "C'mon, you can do this! Let's go. You're the best!" Over and over, she coaches herself about life's possibilities till she believes it.

You can, too. You may feel timid at first, and just whisper at the mirror if you fear the family will guffaw outside the bathroom door. Look yourself in the eye. Start the pep talk. Say how you are, how much confidence you have, and that you're going to make it.

Put some OOMPH in it. Wave your arms. Pat yourself on the head. Act like a winner. Even if you only laugh at your silliness, you will have stomped away your morning blahs.

 The better you feel, the better you'll perform. Grab your pom-poms, strike the pose and cheer yourself to a terrific day.

Winning Strategy #57:

Figure out How Things Work.

G et in the game. No textbooks teach you how to do it; but—as in football—you don't learn from the sidelines. You DO it.

1. As soon as you can, take on low risk, low visibility projects that let you experiment and learn. How do things get done? How do rules get made and broken? How does power really work? You'll skin your knees a few times, but you won't kill your career as you learn.

2. Ask questions. In the beginning, we think the way to seem smart is to act as if we know but say nothing. Actually, question-askers get big credit for intelligence. Organizational truth has varying shades, so ask several people. Discover what feels like *your* truth.

4. Suck up. You have to manage up well, to keep your boss happy, and make sure the top people know who you are. Shy or not, you must put you and your good work forward so BOTH get recognized. Please don't take this suggestion the wrong way. You CAN disagree with your boss (but sensitively and never in public). You will NOT in the long run impress people because you said "Yes, ma'am" and "No, sir" to every higher up. But these are the people who hold your future in their hands. Act like you know that.

3. Shut up. The only way to become a keen observer of people and how things work is to observe. Watch. Keep your counsel. Reflect on what you saw. What did it mean to you? What did you learn from it? Your most powerful teachings are here.

One of the most important things to know in life is how things really work. When you start a job, you must get in the game, ask questions, suck up and shut up.

Winning Strategy #58:

Go Disguised as Yourself.

How many pairs of tap shoes have you worn out since you started working? One or two, because you do a nice shuffle-hop when the boss asks your opinion? Or several dozen because you wear that " love me, love me " smile on your face, and tappity-tappity-tap your shining way into every meeting? Most of us have big shoe bills when we're career babies with few answers to our legions of questions.

People aren't fooled by your "hop-shuffle-step-shuffle-ball-change." Though they tolerate you, they don't like your darling-ness. Nor do they pull you backstage and whisper what the deal is. They let you work frantically to polish the spin designed to hide your doubts and fears of inadequacy, wearing out more shoes. They've handily forgotten their own black patent years.

Give up tap dancing as soon as you can. Let the real and awesome you emerge. Go disguised as yourself—with your real heart and face showing—instead of someone you think the world wants you to be. Others can then venture closer; you'll have more allies; learn and achieve more. You'll glide in more comfortable shoes that take the trail with a surer step; that look and wear better.

Winning Strategy #59:

Just Pay the Man.

Nobody likes paying dues.

You're fresh on the job, maybe just out of college, and full of ideas. To your surprise, people don't listen to you or make you part of the club. They patronize you, put you through humiliating hoops, and don't give you credit for anything. As you gradually gain credibility, you try to put as much distance as you can between dues-paying and you.

Unfortunately, you'll pay dues anytime you're the new kid on the block: You leave your job to get a degree; go to a new industry; change careers; get a new boss. It's hard when others ignore your credentials and hold out a hand for your dues. It only gets harder to do this, never easier. After a few years in the harness, you resent being treated as naive.

You can bulldog through this only if you're the top dog. Otherwise, you get put in puppy class with each beginning. To get through, let people show you what you already know. They don't think you're stupid. THEY want to feel important in YOUR eyes by showing you how smart they are. Be interested and agreeable. They'll eventually see how capable you are.

When you start something new and the dues man comes around, just pay the man.

How can I get good at my job?

Winning Strategy #60:
Figure out the Politics.

P eople either have a nose for politics, sniffing out the nuances of behaviors, or not. If not, office politics is painfully learned and grudgingly played. With or without the nose, your best friends in your early experiences are silence, observation and non-participation. Figure out what's going on and what the rules are before you stick your toe in the water. There are plenty of sharks lurking near your shore willing to grab that toe and make a mess of you.

Experiment to see how you like the game that doesn't have a gameboard, a rulebook that gets written as you go. Feel the pain of losing, the thrill of winning. How thick is your skin? How willing are you to have an adjustable ethic, to even the score, to stomp back at stompers? Can you stay relatively calm, whatever the battle?

Playing politics doesn't mean you become unethical, that you lie or steal, but you do have to accept shifting sands and shades of truth. The people who insist they can maintain a rigid idealism often operate much differently than they say they will. Those who CAN hold themselves above the political fray usually have the money to be able to straddle their high and independent horses.

You need a teacher, another pair of eyes to play this game well. Find someone outside the organization—a school friend who works in the same kind of company, your dad, a career coach—who can help you understand the goings-on, and steer you successfully through shark-infested waters.

You learn this skill through gaffes as well as success, so tread carefully the political path.

Winning Strategy #61:
Go Like Naschke.

Naschke and I went for a walk. He was in his seventies. We had a long, slow way to go this September afternoon. Naschke was a smart man. He spoke several languages. He served in Guam during World War II, his slight body becoming frailer in the tropical heat. He was taken prisoner. He survived.

The war changed him. When he returned home, he decided he never wanted to work for anyone else. He acquired the right to sell newspapers on a downtown corner by the biggest bank in town. Good corner. Naschke sold newspapers for the next 35 years, anonymous to most of his hurrying buyers. He never tried to impress. Whatever his business required, he did it. He worked hard and never got rich, but he was happy because he was doing what he wanted to do. He supported his family, and sent his kids to great universities.

On today's walk, Naschke smiled at my exuberantly youthful stories. A shy man, he had a listening heart. It was a blistering hot day, so we walked slower. We encountered a number of obstacles—high curbs and white-rocked driveways—he just kept going. He didn't shirk or stop or complain. We got to our destination.

Go like Naschke, with a kind heart and up-lifted spirit; and keep going, no matter what.

Winning Strategy #62:
Get a Shadow Consultant.

A shadow consultant saved my bacon. Early in my business, I worked with the president of a company and his vice president son, planning the succession. In our tense, angry sessions, the hard-nosed, dynamic father yelled at his phlegmatic son, and me. I still shiver thinking about that assignment.

I felt out of my league. How could I get a more productive dialogue going? How could they focus on the future instead of each other's throats? I asked the man who taught me about groups. We'd rehash my meeting with the two businessmen and strategize the next. He gave me ideas. He helped me see how I got in my own way.

We eventually effected a smooth transition. I could never have done this without my "shadow consultant." He worked in from the shadows, unknown to the clients, and was a godsend to me.

You too need a shadow consultant, or two or three. They can be people you work with, although it's often better when they're outside your immediate puddle. Pick people who know you, who you view as wise. Don't pick a competitor. Your consultant will ask," What's the problem? What have you done to fix it? Where do you need help?" Your goal is to strategize a solution. Keep in touch with your consultant as you work the plan. Stay with those who give good advice and dump those who don't.

The helper in the shadows can make your light shine brighter.

Winning Strategy #63:
Be Like Ben Harris.

Ben Harris was a remarkable man. Son of a minister, he began his career forty years ago as owner of a tiny photography studio in Oxford, England. His company became successful (and one of the largest in the U.K.) staging and taking group portraits.

Ben was enthusiastic. He jollied others along so they'd catch his energy.

"I love to work," he'd say; "but it's not all fun and, at the end of the day, we want that in our lives, don't we? When I have a task I don't want to do, I make it fun and get it done as quickly as possible. The work will be there whether I like it or not, so I change it in my mind from drudgery to pleasure. That way, I'm always enjoying myself, no matter what I'm doing."

The all-day-every-day perfect job doesn't exist. Even if it's your dream job, you will dislike as much as 30 percent of it. A talented podiatrist trims the bottoms of many callused feet each day. Boring, he says, but, "Tasks like this support me so I can do what I love, the surgeries."

What do you hate about your job? Filing? Going to meetings? Smoothing rough soles? Take a lesson from Ben Harris and face the day with anticipation rather than dread. At the end of it, you'll look back on it with pride and pleasure, not tired bitterness.

Look for ways to make your job fun.

Who can help me figure things out?

Winning Strategy #64:
Tell Somebody Who Cares.

arning: Another commercial.

W Something unsettling happened at work. You don't know who to trust with this one. What should you do?

Tell somebody who cares.

If you seriously want to build a great career, hire a career/life coach. You ask your doctor how to make your body healthy, a stock broker how to make your 401k healthy. Why not ask a career counselor to do the same for your career? The workplace and its politics can be confusing and no classes teach you how to manage your way through that.

Why won't mentors do? They don't always prove helpful. Someone who at first seemed like a good one may not understand your business or you, may be too high in the organization for regular access, may fall from grace and be no help, may believe one conversation should do the trick. Have more than one. Have several informal mentors, and BE one to the folks behind you. Even with that, you need one person to whom you can bare all without fear, someone with sense, who makes you feel good about yourself and encourages your possibilities, who's tough-minded and strategic and been-there, who understands your situation.

 If you already have a mentor/coach relationship with a friend, great! Few people do, though. Visit with a career coach periodically to give you a boost, ideas, a plan. A coach who cares in a can-do way can make your career path smoother.

Winning Strategy #65:
Watch out for Wizards.

In the movie Willow, the High Aldwin holds up his hand. He is about to conduct his annual test. Willow and two other young men want to be his apprentice.

"The power to control the world is in which finger?" he asks them. One hopeful points to the wizard's index finger. Wrong. The next chooses the middle finger. Wrong. Willow hesitates, then picks the ring finger. They are ALL wrong. The Wizard will not have an apprentice this year.

He later asks Willow which finger he had wanted to choose.

"I first thought to pick my own finger," Willow replied. THAT, the High Aldwin tells him, was the right answer.

We are often like Willow and his friends. The powerful-looking stand before us and use words well. We compare their confident stance to our inner fears and conclude they have answers we don't. We devour their words. We give them OUR power. We hope they will save us.

Another wizard lived among the small people of Oz. He met the frequent fate of self-made wizards because a little dog pulled aside a curtain and exposed him—the Great Oz of booming voice and magical promises—as a most ordinary man whose real voice and confused heart were no different than his supplicants'.

Wizards inevitably let us down, and we can become bitter when they do. It's because we want them to give us answers instead of seeking our own.

Richard Nelson Bolles wrote in *What Color Is Your Parachute?* about how to have the work and life you love. It's sold eight million copies! Imagine the wizard-seekers who must hang around after his speeches or write letters asking what they should do with their lives.

I attended one of his annual career planning seminars. We each wanted to KNOW WHAT TO DO. His gentle, but insistent response to us always was, "What do YOU think?"

What do YOU think, Willow? The question seldom has an easy answer, which is why you ask others to guess instead of struggling toward your own discovery. As long as they're wrong—as they often are—you can continue your indecisive floating and avoid the grubbiness of action.

"You have the potential," the High Aldwin said to Willow, "to be a great sorcerer." But, "you must learn to listen to your own heart, to trust your own intuition."

You, like Willow, have considerable wizardry within. Sit in silence and listen for that inner voice which makes up in punch what it lacks in volume. Wisdom lies at the responding end of, "What do I think?"

Don't give up asking for others' counsel. You'll get a fresh perspective or a shape for the idea you couldn't quite give daylight-words to. You must sort through all advice, however, to decide if it feels right for you.

Stop setting up wizards in the first place. Learn to BE your own wizard, and you can stop SEARCHING for one. You'll discover at last how powerful you really are.

How can I get better at my job?

Winning Strategy #66:
Break it Down.

Okay, there's no one older, no book, no information on the Internet about your soon-due project, and you've got to get busy! Still you stare at the blank page, the humming PC screen. How do you get going?

1. Pick the spot. Where do you want to work? In the silence of the conference room? The clatter of the cafeteria? A coffee shop? Your bedroom? Your cubicle after hours? Your office with the calls held? Pick whatever place works for you where you'll be least distracted.

2. Sit in front of the task. You have most likely been doodling, day-dreaming, nail-biting, obsessing; activities that show how absorbed you are by the job to be done, but achieving nothing. Shove aside your other overdue emergencies, turn off the phone, make a commitment of time (an hour? 5 minutes?), and decide what you'll get done in that time. Sitting down and focusing may prove, in the end, to have been the hardest part.

3. Do it by hand. The PC may be your tool of choice, but what if you took up a pen and paper and started writing by hand, moving to the PC when you feel the inner click that says, "I'm cooking'"? I believe we access our creativity better when we start

by hand, where it's easiest, where the creativity can whisper out while you're building confidence in yourself as Project Master.

4. Do something stupid. If you don't have a clue where to start, then begin where you can. Alan Lakein, in *How to Get Control of Your Time and Your Life*, suggests starting with your name, date and project title on the page Those no-brainer tasks may start the flow. If nothing comes, start writing what you don't know. You might be able to switch to what you DO know.

5. Decide where you're going. What are the main PARTS of your project? Scribble the words on a blank piece of paper, in a nice outline or just higgledy-piggledy on the page...Introduction, Conclusions. Findings. Recommendations. Budget. Key Issues. Target Audience. The Plan....whatever needs to be in your proposal/report. Do sub-headings or points occur to you? Include them. In no time you'll have filled the page. This is a rough form of mind-mapping, which is helpful for the creative but terminal procrastinator. It gets you interested in your project and what you have to say.

6. Start where you can. By this time, you're probably engaged, less fearful, ready. Fire up the PC and start capturing your thoughts. Start wherever it feels easiest, where you can say, "OK. Budget categories. At least I can do THAT." Before you know it, you've swirled off into productivity. Your successful beginning AND the looming deadline will probably keep you going.

The secret, says everyone who has nervous-making jobs to do, is to just sit down and do it. Whether you're a writer or a budget analyst, science fiction writer Ray Bradbury's advice applies to you. "To hell with it!" he told a group of aspiring writers. "Get to work!"

Winning Strategy #67:
Get the Monkeys Off Your Back.

Bill Oncken taught people how to manage their time. Not in the efficiency sense, but how to be effective when gorilla bosses go stomping or agendas keep changing or the email is bursting out of your PC.

Those work demands that get in your way of focusing, Oncken called monkeys: "upward-leaping monkeys" if they're your employees," sideways-leaping monkeys" if they're your work pals.

Here's how monkeys operate. You walk down the hall. Someone stops you to ask about a problem. You're not sure what to do, so you say, "Let me think about it and I'll get back to you." According to Oncken, a monkey the other person had been carrying—the problem—just jumped on YOUR back. You now have one more thing to do than before, and this wasn't even on your to-do list!

By the end of the day you could be groaning under the weight of the monkeys who've started building condos on your back because it looks like they'll be there awhile.

When you take on monkeys, it seems reasonable to you. You can do the job better than anyone else (the biggest reason people don't delegate), you don't think fast on your feet, you feel responsible, or that you should help the other. You have a hard time saying "No." Personally, I used to practically offer a ride to every monkey that came my way. It takes time to recognize this isn't compassionate leadership, but bad management.

What do you do with a leaping monkey? Oncken advises, "Hit that SOB in mid-trajectory and send it right back to its owner."

In other words, leave the problem where it belongs, with the other person. Ask questions that leave it there:

"What do YOU think should be done?"

"What have you tried already?"

"Why don't you come up with two or three alternatives and get back to me?"

Let your philosophy be known. One boss put a sign on his desk: "Don't bring me problems, bring me solutions."

Stay standing. You may not escape the monkey entirely, but you can shorten its residency if you stay on your feet and don't accept its leash. Once you sit down, you've changed the encounter to a MEETING and your next hour is COOKED.

You don't do yourself or your people any favors if you solve their problems. They don't learn, and you don't get hero points. You just get tired.

You can't always swat away monkeys. Bosses get to give you monkeys ("downward-leaping monkeys") and you're smart to take them. In the informal economy of the workplace, at least sharing the leash peers try to hand you is necessary in creating your help network, sort of an ongoing monkey lend-lease program. You will never have total control of your time, but you'll be better all around if you splash a little monkey repellent on your face each morning.

Winning Strategy #68:
Help the Boss Lighten the Grip.

How do you get your boss to delegate more responsibility to you? You won't, if you have a boss who micromanages. That boss never trusts any employee, has to have her thumbprint on everything, and as a result runs an unproductive organization, which is her fault, but she sees herself as having lousy employees, which causes her to micromanage more! Get the picture?

Not all bosses are like that. In fact, they can be *too* ready to let go of responsibility, and check on the progress of projects *too* infrequently, and that means you can find yourself in alligator-infested waters before the boss realizes she needs to bring in her sharpshooter gear.

The boss who's reluctant to delegate is usually new at the boss job or new to you (and doesn't know you well enough to let go). Here's how you change that: Think of yourself as the total manager of this project and completely organize it, preferably step by step, on paper. What's needed to get the job done, in terms of people or other resources? What are necessary checkpoints so the boss doesn't get too out of touch with it?

Show this to the boss. Your project walkthrough may not be perfect, but it will show the boss how you would tackle it, and she'll give you pointers that will help you avoid the swamp. Because bosses can be so overwhelmed with projects, your outline may be just the thing to convince her to let you try your organizational wings on it (the checkpoints will help raise her comfort level).

Once you've done a few projects successfully, with only minor screw-ups, additional freedom usually comes.

What about loyalty and trust?

 *Winning Strategy #69:*

Give Crowns and Pounds.

A poetical interlude:

> When I was one-and-twenty
>   I heard a wise man say,
> "Give crowns and pounds and guineas
>   But not your heart away;
> Give pearls away and rubies
>   But keep your fancy free."
> But I was one-and-twenty,
>   No use to talk to me.
>
> When I was one-and-twenty
>   I heard him say again,
> "The heart out of the bosom
>   Was never given in vain;
> 'Tis paid with sighs a-plenty
>   And sold for endless rue."
> And I am two-and-twenty,
>   And oh, 'tis true, 'tis true."
>
> —A. E. Housman

It's painful to put your love (or loyalty) in the wrong place.

How loyal can you be? On the one hand, we LIKE aligning ourselves with an organization or cause. We were taught to be loyal to our friends and beliefs. Our company seems a natural loyalty depository. On the other hand is the reality of today's workplace, increasingly run by the numbers, where people get discarded as quickly as wet nose tissue. You would be stooopid to fly your "Loyalty Forever" flag over a cubicle you know they'll snatch from you in a few months. The poet's "sighs a-plenty" and "endless rue" would be yours as you got downsized out of the building.

Make it part of your job-search checklist to find a place where loyalty matters. Many employers (especially entrepreneurial firms) value loyalty, sometimes too much so. If your 120 percent effort gets rewarded with money, position, and a little security, you'll be happier, more inclined to help and less inclined to walk away at the first ominous breeze.

Companies pay big-time for ho-humming loyalty. When the message is, "We need you now, but don't count on our retirement plan," employees say, "I got it," and respond accordingly, with their feet. (Employee retention is a huge problem because. . .?) If a company you want to work for hasn't realized the value of a loyal you, go there for the experience, the exposure or the money, but

> "Give crowns and pounds and guineas
> But not your heart away."

Guard your loyalty. Give it to the business to the extent it's given to you. Stay light-footed and ready to leave. If you are too loyal, you'll rue having given away your heart and gotten so little back.

Winning Strategy #70:
Learn Who to Trust.

Trust is the coin of the realm in business, and it is vital that you be trustworthy and honest. You don't think so at first, as the slick guys whiz past you, unencumbered by stodgy ethics, and always winning. At the end, however, they will have slid screaming down their slimy road to oblivion, and reliable you will still stand. They won't have a helping hand to break the fall because they stomped on too many as they whizzed along.

Okay, you're trustworthy. How much can you trust others? You can generally trust people till they reach the boundary of their self-interest. Then they DO take care of themselves, and they should. Survival is our strongest instinct. We learn we MUST watch out for ourselves and not be like the foolish fox.

A scorpion finagled a ride across a raging river from his reluctant natural enemy, the fox.

"You'll sting me," said the wary fox.

The scorpion soothed the redhead: "Why would I sting you? We'd both die."

"Why?" wailed the fox in midstream, drowning after the scorpion stung him.

"How could you expect me not to be me?" burbled the also-dying bug.

Be grateful for people's nobility and generosity, which you'll receive in the measure you give it to them; but if you demand it or expect more than their self-interest dictates, you won't.

You learn who NOT to trust by harvesting the arrows in your back and reading the nameplate on the shaft. Trust with the heart of a child, but not the mind of a fool. Watch others' behavior. If they honor your trust, hand out more; if they trash it, take it away. You can still work with them; you'll just understand better how they play the game. At the end of your career, you'll have just a handful of totally trustworthy cohorts, and that'll be okay.

CHAPTER
5

Get Ahead

Y ou gaze at the career ladder before you, the higher rungs shrouded in fog. You're not sure how far you can or want to go, but you have that divine dissatisfaction, that unwillingness to stay in place.

Before you spit on your hands, grasp the rails and take that next step up, read this. It'll chase away some of the fog.

What's the best way to succeed?

Winning Strategy #71:

Get a Raise.

D o you get regular performance reviews and an annual increase? Whether you like the amount or the fairness of distribution among good and bad performers, you get raises. You may get a bonus based on goals achievement or have a contract that spells out your salary.

This tip is not for you. This is for those in the small company or family-owned business where whim or distraction, not policy, often governs. How do you get a raise?

Look first at how well the business is doing. If today's balance sheets and tomorrow's prospects look grim, don't bother. Next consider the owner or manager. What kind of person is he? What moves him? What does he need to see before making a decision? (What the owner responds to is key.)

Now, what in your performance suggests a raise is warranted? What contributions have you made? Customers brought in? Cash saved? Your strongest argument will be how you've helped the business prosper. Write this down. Include financial or other data.

Fairness issues are second-level arguments, but develop them anyway. How long has it been since you've gotten a raise? How do you compare with others in the company or the competition (and how hot would you be in the marketplace? Tread carefully here. You don't want the boss to say, "So, go!") Write this down.

Having looked at both, now decide what you're asking for. How much? When? Do you want cash? Will you settle for perks? Be specific. Have a fallback position, a lesser amount that still seems fair.

Call the front sheet "Performance Achievements" and the second "Additional Information" or something similar. Use bullet point statements, not impassioned pleas. Focus on business logic, not emotion.

Tell the boss you want a meeting to review your salary, that you'll cover the specifics then. At the meeting, present the two sheets, get his reaction. Does he agree? Is he angry? You want to know where he stands. Don't be surprised if he says, "Let me think about it." Push for a back-together date.

Don't let this drop; but realize this will probably get delayed several times. Get another meeting. Get his agreement and an amount. If he won't say but asks you, be aware that a typical increase is between 1 and 5%. If he has to correct a gross inequity and give more than that, he'll want to space it out, unless losing you is imminent. Go ahead and ask, be prepared to be negotiated back, but not—I hope—all the way to your fallback position.

This is, as you might imagine, a dreadful task. You'll get huge sweat moons under your armpits from taking on what you correctly believe is the boss' job. But you'll feel great if you succeed.

Don't wait, don't whine. Start working on your two sheets. It's a shame that getting a raise requires this, but it might.

Winning Strategy #72:

Have an Hour of Power.

Y ou want to concentrate on work; but phones ring; meetings and problems intrude, and days end with exhaustion, not pride. How can you control your time?

Go to your office an hour early one day and prowl the halls. The lit-up cubicles will be occupied by the ambitious, the going-places people. They're having their Hour of Power. This is when they can work without interruptions. They have fresh energy, the opportunity to think, to work on goals, to organize projects and people. By the time the clock-watchers roll in, the earlybirds have moved their careers ahead a significant notch.

Take 30 minutes if you can't do an hour. If you're comatose till the coffee break but cookin' at 5:30 PM, stay late and make that your Hour of Power. Avoid saying, "I'll work late at home." The bulging briefcase often sits by the front door, and leaves —untouched—for work next morning. If you can't leave for work when the early birds are chirping, wake up early and work in a quiet corner away from the family.

The hour makes a difference. If you're not willing, then re-think your ambition. Success needs an Hour of Power to be more than a pipedream.

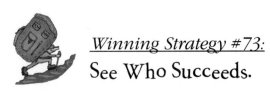

Winning Strategy #73:
See Who Succeeds.

W e begin our career craving success. We want to make it to the top. Drive zips in us. We are all promise on the outside, with a little terror on the inside. What does it take to succeed? Who makes it to the top?

(Some don't have grand ambitions. Their job may be "just a job" that supports a family or interesting non-work activities. Career ladders don't entice them.)

Those shaped by dreams and dissatisfaction with the status quo reach for the stars. It's the artist who must create, the business owner captivated by the daily scurry, the sales rep motivated by money, the executive happily sweating at the corporate game. Can you tell at the starting gate who'll win the prize? For two decades I've watched climbers hack away at the mountain of success, and here are my observations.

It isn't the brightest kid. School-smart people can be undisciplined because they don't have to apply themselves in class, and can't when they hit the workplace. The highly intelligent don't always live up to the potential everyone thought they had. Brilliant people may drive cabs and work in factories because it makes them happy or the life of the mind appealed more than political goings-on. It isn't the obvious stars. The success mountain is littered with novas that flared bright but flamed out early, who had little more substance than their press releases.

Raw ambition succeeds...the woman so ambitious she'd step over her mother's body to achieve a goal. Like everyone, she sometimes fail at endeavors, but she'll get right back at it.

Middling, quiet people also succeed, and they're the surprises. They may not initially impress; but one day there they are, standing on a mound of stardust detritus. How do they do that?

1. Successful people do their jobs and take on extra ones. They do their job...plus. They're willing to do the jobs the boss wants done.

2. They focus on relationships. They lunch with the comers and the never-wills. They get outside their department or function. They play softball with the Purchasing Department "girls." They call the accountant who just lost her baby. They attend their secretary's wedding. They share any limelight. Over time, they can get anything done because they have relationships everywhere.

They avoid battles between titans, but have friends in both camps. They survive purgings. They may prefer solitude, but never forget the people quotient. True loners succeed only as long as their extraordinary work produces extreme money.

3. Successful people focus and persist. They understand that you get things done through others. I feel sorry for people with Attention Deficit Disorder (ADD) because butterflies can lure them from the grind, along a lush green path, and they forget their way home. Successful people keep their suitpants in the chair, their minds on the deadline. When you admire the glamorous director or opera star, remember that their years at the grind of endless tape reviews or singing scales got them here.

4. Successful people create "completion" combinations. We're all limited as human beings. This is how people with ADD do get to the top. They can't focus, so they partner with people who do. They don't bemoan what they're NOT or try to change what they can't. The ADD entrepreneur marries Structure woman. The

peripatetic DJ hires a manager. The flamboyant sales rep partners with the detail-loving customer service assistant.

These partnerships have conflict potential because each player brings different values. The sales personality sees the financial type as stodgy, while the latter sees the former as a gladhander. They succeed when they stifle critical feelings, appreciate differing abilities and focus on the goal.

5. Successful people understand their limits. They know what's "not me," and they say "No," albeit judiciously. They don't overcommit.

6. They have a sense of urgency, a "What's the matter with today?" attitude. They want the job done NOW.

7. Successful people have charisma. They may be shy. They may not slap backs or tell raunchy jokes; they may seldom smile. But there's something about them. They understand the heart, what inspires it and how to motivate it. People WANT to follow them

Your organization may not see you as a star, but if you have these qualities, success may indeed be yours. Keep plugging.

Winning Strategy #74:
See What They Want.

How do you make sense of people getting promoted? What did they have that the company liked? How do you know if you have it?

Pay little attention to company career development policies. The organization wants the chirpy, fair-minded statement to be true, but the person who hands out the promotions didn't write the copy.

Focus instead on who heads the company and what behaviors get rewarded. Are you led by marketers, bean-counters or techies? They reward what they value. So, if you're a marketer in a technology-focused company, go get more computer skills. If you're a techno-wizard working for a bean-counter, design programs that paint the bottom line in rainbow colors and learn how to say "value-added."

Look at the people the company is rewarding now. What THEY have (whether you like it or not) is what YOU need to get.

Look where the company is headed. Can you identify skills the future will require? Don't be a knee-jerk chaser of fields that aren't YOU, but if the company is acquiring chemical companies, you'll benefit from talking with synthetic organic chemists to understand the business of science, AND some science. If it's becoming more technologically oriented, sign up for computer classes. You want to have what the company wants when the company needs it.

Winning Strategy #75:
Step Off the Ledge.

In the film, "Indiana Jones and the Last Crusade," adventurer/ archeologist Indiana Jones (Harrison Ford) searches for his father, Professor Henry Jones (Sean Connery), on a quest to find the Holy Grail. It holds the gift of everlasting life to anyone who drinks from it.

The professor is found, they're on the Grail trail, and they've survived Nazis, fires, rides in tanks that topple over cliffs. Indy learns there are three final challenges once they locate the cave where an ancient knight guards the cup. The professor translated the riddle:

"The breath of God. Only the penitent man will pass."

"The word of God. In the footsteps of God will he proceed."

"The path of God. In a leap from the lion's head will he prove his worth."

They reach the cave. Nazis shoot Indy's father, who will die if he doesn't get the Grail's healing waters. Indiana makes it through the first two trials. As he passes a lion's head, he comes to the cave's exit, from which drops a wide bottomless chasm, across which is the entrance to the cave with the cup. Impossible to cross.

His father moans in pain. Indy has no choice. This will take a leap of faith. He closes his eyes and steps forward. He doesn't topple into vast nothingness; his foot hits solid stone! Suddenly the camera angle shifts and we see what no one could before, that a thick stone bridge connects the caves. This optical illusion has always persuaded the less courageous to turn back. You had to take the step to know it was there.

Indiana tosses small white stones onto the bridge and the pathway becomes obvious. He gets the Grail, saves his father and beats the bad dudes.

Your life is like that cave. Danger snarls at you from behind. Help feels out of reach. Lives may be at stake. The fear-ridden show you the warning label: Stepping out of caves into apparently bottomless caverns can be hazardous to your health. You'll meet more of these than Indiana Joneses. They cling to their cave walls. They don't even assess the risks or venture forward.

Sometimes you just gotta step out in faith. Find handholds, but dreams worth having require a breathless, teeth-chattering decision to step out into the void. As Indy discovered, you may be surprised to find rock-solid support for the chance you took.

Go ahead. Make a leap of faith.

Winning Strategy #76:
Hang Out With Fast Girls.

To move faster on your career path, hang out with the fast girls. Look around the company. You can easily see who the fast girls (and boys) are. No, they're not the ones your mom didn't want you to bring home in high school because they had bad habits and loose morals. I'm talking about the people you admire, who seem to be getting things done, going places. They are not necessarily the ones scrambling for the top.

Who around you is approaching work is an admirable way? Who seems on the ball to you, or just a bit better than you at the job? Ally yourself with people like this, who'll make you want to stretch, try a little harder. In playing tennis: you find a player better than you; not out of your league, but good enough to make you play your best.

You might not want to. You feel more secure when you're the lead dog in the pack. Pity. You learn more when you surround yourself with people who can help you improve. And the synergy of those combined abilities can get more done than you imagined possible. Gives you a rush, too, to be in an environment like that.

We can, if left without that friendly challenge, sink into a morass of lethargic lobs or ineffectual charging at the net. Being with others on a faster road to somewhere picks up your pace, exercises your capabilities, makes you feel breathless but great at the end of a day.

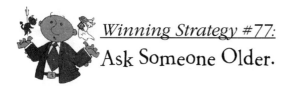

Winning Strategy #77:
Ask Someone Older.

Lou is a successful real estate developer. He was so poor as a child, his family slept under a farm truck! He worked in shipyards and the poultry business, became an entrepreneur who had gas stations and laundromats and then cast an eye on real estate development, where he wanted to make his mark...and he did...big time. How had he managed to come this far?

"I had nothing," he told me. "I knew nothing and no one. So I figured out the only way to learn this business was to look at the successful guys in this business. Whatever they did, I did."

We agonize alone about how to solve our unique and surely insurmountable problems. We fail to look around or up, to see if anyone has already solved it (and someone frequently has). Asking feels like cheating; we're supposed to figure things out ourselves.

Someone I loved dearly was entering the work world. Oh, the pain, the missteps my advice could save her. I showered her with my counsel. She leveled me with a gaze and told me, like the Joker in "Batman" said after his wife's admiring remark, "I didn't ask."

I shut up and she made her own way. We all want our own imprint on our lives, but if you can overcome your prickly need to whistle "I did it my way," look at successful people and ask how they did it. One of my smartest clients does. He zeroes in on people ten years older than he, the ones just ahead of him on the journey. He asks how they achieved particular successes AND what they would do differently.

the Point

To grow farther faster, find people already scarred. Ask whether they can show you a better route through life's brambles.

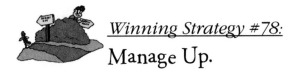

Winning Strategy #78:
Manage Up.

As bosses go, he was the sleaze of unethical sleazes. You name it, he was it: a political dog, predator of women, liar. You'd leave a meeting with him and wish you could bathe. But he taught me a valuable lesson: the importance of managing up.

I hadn't been doing that, of course. I had this Champion of the People thing going; I thought it my duty to defend them, challenge him, help him see the righter path; oh, and do a great job.

No, no, my little chickadee, he counseled. "It's fine to turn in a good performance and achieve those goals," (waving a hand at my notes), "but the most important thing to get right is to make your boss happy." This wasn't a come-on. He was telling me that I should be doing what mattered to HIM, and only secondarily to ME. What were HIS needs? What would make HIM look good, take care of HIS emergencies, give him chits with HIS boss? And, sweetie, he hinted, you're not getting high marks from me.

I left his office in search of a washcloth, indignant at this slimy advice; but over time as I've waved the boss's wand myself, I've agreed with him. When I've mentally lined up my best-ever employees, I didn't pick the ones struggling into Joan of Arc armor, but those who had "How can I help you today, oh Great One?" sensibilities. It wasn't a mewling sycophancy, but a feeling my urgencies were shared. "Let me change evening plans so we can get the job done," or "I'll run interference to keep you from the rat hole you're about to tumble into."

Be careful adopting this necessary attitude. Your taking care of the boss is the pendulum's first swing. The next is how the boss takes care of you in return. If she gives you your head and lets you prance, then your managing-up super-efforts are worth it. But if your lathering mouth and worn out hooves don't even net you a blanket after the race, then this is the wrong racetrack. You need to go someplace where they'll run you hard, but treat you like a champion in return.

Managing up means to give up some of your idealism, but your whole career is an exercise in exchanging youthful black-and-white, high contrast ideals for the variegated grays of reality. If you can't, then good luck finding the occupation that doesn't require managing up. Ignoring the uncomfortable truths of organizational life keeps you lower in the food chain or headed to the sole practitioner's stall.

 Carry the boss's banner. I hope it takes you to the winner's circle.

Winning Strategy #79:
Do Whatever It Takes.

He is a filmmaker, just back from Hawaii where lava fumes ate his camera and he's a third shy of the money he needs to complete his film. He is tense and focused elsewhere. He is the son of his father, a tireless entrepreneur. When asked to take on challenges, the dad would say, "That's impossible. It's never been done;" but the first to add, "Let's try it!"

The filmmaker has that same willingness to do whatever it takes to reach a desired goal. I see it in clients all the time. He's a broadcaster who has to make tricky, risky calls, and does. She's a mogul-in-training and gets an assignment that stretches her to tears most days, but she hangs in. He's in finance and wants appointments with me early or late so he can figure out how to get his groove back. If focus on the task means anything—and it does—they'll get what they want.

You can see it in living color if you go to a parent-child information meeting at a coveted college campus where the student has a 5 percent or less chance of getting in. "Whatever it takes" whips around the room among these ambitious families, like the snitch at Harry Potter's Quidditch game.

You can see it in small ways too, like the woman who always got up before dawn, her infant son's rise-and-shine time. "I just need an hour for myself, before taking care of him and going off to work," she told me. It's no surprise she put it to work in bigger things. She owns several restaurants today.

Having "whatever it takes" to power your goal-engine doesn't guarantee success. But a filmmaker's focus, a financier's determination and a mom's discipline often takes you beyond what talent alone can achieve. How does yours measure up?

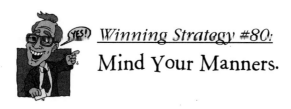

Winning Strategy #80:

Mind Your Manners.

Vince Bommarito owns Tony's, a world-class, award-winning restaurant in St. Louis. Going to Tony's is an EVENT, from coat-check to postprandial liqueur. The waiters pamper. Vince himself loves to make a happiness check around the room, to sprinkle cheese on the pasta and smooth the crisp linen. All is perfection. The salad is PRESENTED; the desserts have a pedigree.

How does Vince choose his waiters, those maestros in a tux whose job it is to give you an experience that's worth the price of the ticket?

"They need two things," Vince says. "Attitude and manners. If they have that, I can teach them the rest. If they don't, they can never do this job."

You may not aspire to be wait-staff at a prestigious restaurant, but Vince's philosophy is shared by lots of bosses. If you have the right attitude, you'll get ahead. Period. If you have a bad one—no matter how talented you are—you may not get heaved out, but you'll certainly put a drag on your career parachute.

A bad attitude can be the basis for a bad performance evaluation. The boss often can't articulate how you fell short, may be too timid to call you on your attitude. Yes, you performed the job duties, but you were hard to manage. You took too much psychic energy. You were negative about new ideas; you may have been right, but managed to make others feel stupid or angry on the way. You complain a lot. You never speak up at meetings, but you spread the sabotaging word afterwards. You claim to hate politics, but you practice a malevolent brand of it. These behaviors spring from a bad attitude.

A good attitude, on the other hand, conveys: I'm here in mind and heart. I'm ready. I'm available. I'm willing to go the extra mile. I can change and adapt. I can learn. I'm on the team. I'm part of something important that must get done.

Good manners isn't simply knowing which is the pickle fork. It's showing respect, regard and consideration for the other guy, an acknowledgement that achievement generally requires many key players, a willingness to share the glory, to treat human beings as if they have the same greatness you do. This kind of "manners" goes deeper than any etiquette book, and it nicely crosses cultures.

If your attitude says, "Yes" and your manners say "ma'am," you can go just about as far as you want in an organization. Stay lost in your snarly rudeness, however, and you'll never be able to afford Tony's, but will be dining at Happy Jack's at a table for one.

Keep your attitude up and your manners showing.

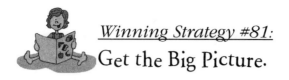

Winning Strategy #81:
Get the Big Picture.

You're sitting at a meeting, perky and straight-backed, notepad ready. As the agenda whips along, something meaningful whizzes back and forth but you're not sure what it is. You study the others' behavior - the shrugs, knowing glances, restless feet. Wha'? Huh? What's going on?

One of the scarred soldiers next to you takes pity and whispers what the true agenda is and what you're really here to do. Oh. So I'm NOT here as a member of the TEAM-Yes! Advisory Council to bring employee concerns to the Executive Committee. I'm supposed to love the program the vice president will present.

It's your first lesson in getting the bigger picture. You learn by watching, asking, testing, getting it wrong, and in other ways expanding your understanding of what isn't written down. It requires most of your pores and all of your senses. Don't go to the bookstore. This text will never be written.

The more you understand the big picture, the more you get to play. The less you get it, the longer you stay in a lower place, where you can pay attention to minutia, to doing your job well but in a silo, to the rigid following of rules and procedures. The saddest fact is that the good-job-doers bitterly wonder why their exceptional performance loses out to the just-okay gladhanders who get the promotions. They couldn't see beyond the details; they don't get it; and no amount of explanation satisfies.

the Point

Yes, you should do your job well; and yes, God is in the details; but getting ahead requires you to open that Big Picture book ever wider.

What harsh realities lie on the road to success?

Winning Strategy #82:
Don't Watch the Sausage

L ife is different at the top.

German Chancellor Otto von Bismarck said: "The making of sausage and laws do not bear watching." The stomach, apparently, finds both hard to take.

Also gruesome when observed: high-level meetings to plan raising major funds for a charity, decision-making at the top level, and making big money. It's all brass knuckles here, and these children don't play well with others. This is where the rubber hits the road, where the game is serious, and no fluffy corporatespeak buffers the reality. The battle is won or lost at these board games, and the players know it. Only the tough of mind and stomach need apply.

Aspirants tell their bosses they want to make it to the top. They work hard to get there, eager for the prestige, the perks, the company jet. They don't realize the executive suite isn't as clubby as the middle management nest.

One day they arrive and they see how life works here. You don't see friendly competition, but fiefdoms headed by a sword-brandishing warlord snarling for the support of dukes (and a few duchesses), who rattle sabers back at him. Despite the speeches some underling wrote for their annual holiday meeting address about "servant leadership," it doesn't even have a file drawer here. Nor does fairness. If you aren't agile, you can get flayed or caught in a crossfire with poison darts. What you did yesterday doesn't matter. You're in or out of the game and the stakes are high. More than one client, newly arrived at this terrorist-proof wing, has fled the game's brutality for friendlier campfires.

(This is not, by the way, a diatribe against executives, fund raisers or money makers. In fact, the most interesting game is here. The air is alive with risk and combat. Companies are built, jobs get created, families get supported. I like playing there.)

As you trudge the good-soldier ranks, know what awaits you at the top. The guys who write management books have almost never been there. The guys who live it don't write well about it.

If the top level is what you want, go to a pig farm one autumn Saturday. Listen to the squeals. Observe the cauldrons. Heft the tools. Wade around in the rubber boots. Then decide whether sausage-making in the executive suite is truly your career dream.

CHAPTER 6

Get Out of Career Jail

Not all days are sunny in the old Workday Corral. The boss snarls. Your company loses money and everyone blames you. You find it hard to muster the old "what-ho!" for your servitude. In short, there's trouble in paradise.

Life in every organization has problems. Despite your best efforts, you sometimes fail. You even look at your dream job from time to time and hate it. What do you do when you lose your enthusiasm, when you screw up or the boss doesn't like you, or you get passed over or demoted? Is this just a bad Monday, or is evil afoot? Are you being pushed out the door? Do you need new horizons? What kind of trouble are you in? How do you get out of it? Do you or somebody else think it's time for you to go?

Here are a few handholds.

**What do you do
when you don't like your job anymore?**

Winning Strategy #83:

Sing that Song with Feelin'.

In the movie "Groundhog Day," Bill Murray plays a self-centered TV weatherman who travels to Punxsutawney, Pennsylvania to cover Groundhog Day. Will Groundhog Phil see his shadow on February 2? After the ceremonies, a blizzard forces Murray back to the town he couldn't wait to leave, and to the same hotel where, the next morning, the deejays' patter is the same! Murray discovers he's trapped in a time warp and it's February 2 again. He flees town that afternoon, a blizzard forces him back, and next day—February 2!

Ever felt stuck in Groundhog Day? Where the days have relentless predictability? Where you feel head-bangingly bored or too hip for the room, but unable to escape? What do you do when you make too much money to leave, or when this job is the only one you can get, or you're too scared to risk something new?

1. Tell somebody! If you can, tell people who matter at your work how you feel. The confession can lead to assignments that bust up boredom's logjam. If you fear the revelation could lead to the back door and the shredding of your I.D. badge, keep it to yourself. But take out SOMEBODY you trust for coffee and pour out your heart. You'll feel better; you may also get helpful suggestions.

2. Re-invent yourself. Larry had worked in a family business 20 years. He longed for an end to his tedium, but the photo of his young children kept him chained to his desk. He re-invented himself. He lost weight; grew his hair long; started going on skiing trips alone; went into therapy to learn how to make himself happier in place. He stopped wearing suits.

3. Re-invent the job. He also made his job more interesting. He tried each day to look at it with new eyes. He created his company's first strategic plan; became more involved in the community as spokesman for his firm. He moved his office furniture so it faced sun streaming in the factory's windows. He scoured every inch of the place to find new challenges and opportunities along a track that, basically, would not change. He became a happier man.

4. Do something nice for someone else. Few things make you feel worse than "Forever February 2." A sure cure for misery like this is to put it in perspective. Find someone with a lousier life than yours and give of yourself. Help a friend down on her luck; take food to a homeless shelter; organize a fund-raiser for a child with a head injury. Acting with love for others will remind you how lucky you are. Your situation won't seem as grim.

5. Sing that song with feelin'. Country singer Jerry Lee Lewis sang: "Ya gotta sing that song with feelin', boy, after all the feelin's gone." How many times did he do "Great Balls o' Fire," or Rod Stewart "Maggie May," or Mick Jagger "Satisfaction"? About a thousand times more than they wanted, you may be sure. You have to be a professional, no matter how bored you are. You have to jump on stage and sing your song with the enthusiasm you had just after you wrote it. It's why your fans pay you.

6. Remind yourself why you're doing this. What brought you to this job? What passion drove you? If you can recall why you got on this road, maybe you can whiskbroom away boredom's sand and re-discover the yellow brick road beneath a parched desert.

Get outside yourself and work to fix your woes if you're stuck in Groundhog Day. Bill Murray learned compassion, growth and love. I wish the same for you.

How do get out of career trouble?

Winning Strategy #84:
Don't Bleed.

wonderful, often-copied "primer" on swimming with sharks gets passed around offices. The first rule is: don't bleed. You'll only attract other sharks.

It's true. What a shock when you first learn that those nice people you work with can be vicious, that they don't play by the rules, and that you're interesting to hunt. Sharks become more numerous the higher you go in the organization. It's what often sends fishlets away from the upper management rapids and back to the predictable confines of the fish tank. The game gets too bloody.

You HAVE to learn shark behavior. If you're testing your baby fins, don't move around much. Content yourself to idle on the sidelines and see who they bite and how. Who carries off the bleeding prey? Who gets carried off to Sea World? If you're inexperienced, don't get in the pond. The only shark repellent I know is to be the boss' kid, and that only works when the boss is looking. Otherwise, your posterior is just as bitable as everyone else's.

You also have to learn whether you can be a sharklet. A low-tech, low-risk way to test your sharkiness is to become involved in community organizations. You may get hurt here, but not in the costlier way it will happen at work, where the bites go deeper, all the way to your pocketbook. Get on the planning committee. Run for P.T.A. sergeant-at-arms. Protest some big business chewing up your village parkland. It doesn't matter what the office or cause is. It's all a shark training pool.

The waters are murky, roiling. You don't know what's up or who your friend is or where the undertows are. Friend today is foe tomorrow and back again. What you thought was justice makes someone else call you foul. The quietest fish often have the most fatal bite. It is difficult to know what "right" is, much less do it. If swimming here invigorates you, then community and/or office politics may be your bag. If shifting alliances, drifting sands and unfair advantages make you seasick, better stay on land.

 Swimming with sharks is not for bleeders or the fainthearted.

Winning Strategy #85:
Take a Tour of Career Hell.

You stagger from your annual review, stunned. Surely you'll awaken from this nightmare and be the fair-haired child once more. Your boss just told you you've failed on major goals; that your staff complains about you as manager. You ask for specifics and you get vague, puzzling superficialities. That project was cancelled, the budget withdrawn. Why is this a big deal? What happened to the praise for my glorious achievements? The boss ho-hums you out the door.

You brood for several days then write a long rebuttal, to which the boss doesn't respond. You're so shocked and angry you go to Human Resources who shunts you back with a policy that you can request a hearing with the boss' boss. You get the session, but the *uber*-weasel supports your weasel boss.

Overnight your life changes. Your treasured independence vanishes and you're micro-managed. Your staff—even your assistant!—is taken away, but your goals remain at a high, now unreachable level. Your boss holds weekly meetings with you "to help you get back on track" that are Kafka-esque exercises. You thought you'd done exactly what you were told, but your boss routinely explodes. "That wasn't at ALL what I wanted!"

You get diarrhea and can't sleep at night. You work harder on perfection for just one, "Good job!" You never get it. You become belligerent. Your boss sends uncooperative you to HR, who sends you to the EAP (employee assistance program) so you get your right attitude back. Three months into this, the boss sadly pronounces, "This isn't working," and hints you may soon be on probation.

Welcome to Career Hell. You are living in one of the most despicable management practices in the manual. The truth is, there's nothing wrong with you. You haven't changed. The organization has, in these kinds of ways: The top gun wants a different team. The board adopted the latest management fad, and your job is redundant. You have a new boss and the chemistry is bad. What makes it so awful is its dishonesty and its killing effect on the human soul. It is also almost completely effective.

You get put on probation, and within 90 days you're generally gone because—not knowing what you did wrong in the first place —you don't know how to fix it. Bitter, stressed out, shell-shocked, you either resign in the threat of being fired or you stick out your glass chin and they deliver the knockout punch, escorting you out the door in front of your peers, your personal worth tossed into the cardboard box the security guard watched you pack before marching you out like the pariah you've become.

Now try to smile confidently at your next interview.

Your naiveté played a part here, your nose-to-the-grindstone trust that quid will get you quo. You didn't see this coming, you didn't know the scheme, you couldn't see a way out and you fell under its crushing pressure. Almost everybody does.

You may also have played a role here. Was it time for you to go and you were afraid to acknowledge the signs? The next chapter's "Know When It's Time to Go" tells you how to recognize when you need new pastures. Here, we'll assume it was the organization's crummy idea of a chess game. What do you do if this happens to you?

1. Think twice about going to HR. That function serves two masters, the company AND the employees, and the goals don't always mesh. My clients often find them, in this situation, "out of the loop," "not to be trusted," "part of the strategy". My hope is that you'd find a trusted counselor who could help, but make sure one occupies that seat before you open the HR gate.

2. Get help. If you have a friend in HR elsewhere (and she *gets* it), ask her advice. See a lawyer who specializes in employment law (for the plaintiff—*you*—not the employer). Generally, you don't have grounds for action, but it's worth paying for the hour. Call somebody like me who can help steer through this skunkworks, keep you from a tailspin toward depression and performance decline, who can help develop a strategy and stay on it.

3. Assess your organizational muscle. You will almost certainly be booted out the door. I've seen this situation reverse itself only when (a) the boss himself was on shaky ground, (b) the employee had bigger friends in higher places than the boss, (c) the person had the pluck and luck to wait out the storm; poof! the organization changed and all was well again (never count on this), or (c) the company feared an attention-getting lawsuit and bad press.

4. Get ready to leave. This juggernaut is relentlessly effective. You will have a tendency to stand like a deer in the headlights or a defendant pounding his innocence before a hangin' judge. Forget it. Blink those eyes, gather your wits, shut up, get moving and heave the self-pity into the ocean. You have a career to save.

The most likely outcome is your departure six months down the road. You can go out with some of your self-esteem intact and maybe something from the company, too. Clients have gotten: Resignation with a letter of recommendation and record expungement. Time off to look for another job; essentially being relieved of most duties, including the weekly thumb-wrenching meetings. Services of an outplacement firm and (occasionally) severance pay when they need to buy your silence and good will or it's in a contract you have with the company.

Remind yourself daily it is the company, not you. You no longer fit but they lack the honesty and/or the heart to help you out a necessary door.

Winning Strategy #86:

Pass Over Passed Over.

You do a great job, but got passed over for a promotion. Why? In choosing the best person for the job, companies use a set of criteria and you probably didn't meet them. Just because you do a good job, you are not automatically in line.

Ask your boss why you got passed over. I'll be surprised if you get a straight answer, however. "We picked the best qualified person," most bosses say. The inexperienced boss will give you a list of what you don't have.

Too often the passed-over employee WORKS on that list then says, "Here, I did what you told me. NOW give me the promotion." You won't get it, the boss won't say why, and you'll stay unhappy.

But if you TRAINED the person who got the job, why wouldn't YOU get the promotion? You may ONLY have technical competence and not the "soft" aspects that matter.

Your boss won't tell you, but she might think this: I don't like you. You don't fit the management team. The chemistry's bad. You're not the right age/race/gender. You're great at the technical pieces, but lousy at the people part. You can't see the bigger picture.

If you get passed over several times, do you have a chance? Within the current management structure, you'll have a difficult time.

I've known plenty of people who've gotten their promotion because:

1. They outlasted the management, and the new management saw them as promotable; OR

2. They've gone to another company, gotten bigger and different experience, and then come back to the old company in an even HIGHER position.

Don't have blinders on, but don't lose hope either. Change if you can, but look outside the company for other opportunities.

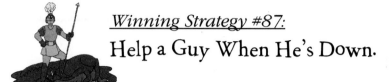

**Winning Strategy #87:**
Help a Guy When He's Down.

The room feels dark, oppressive. Your heart has thudded into your shoes. Slack-jawed and dead-eyed, you watch your colleagues trudge out of the room, avoiding your eyes. You screwed up, big-time and in public. Nowhere to run, nowhere to hide from this failure.

From the shadows steps a silent angel, silent because what words at this point have balm? Angel because she is there to pick up the body parts and put you back together. She helps you gather bits of the exploded project, folds a flap of flayed flesh back in place, and tidies up your bloodied battleground. She stays at your elbow so you'll stay away from sharp edges. She penetrates the gloom of your cave where you've gone to lick your wounds. Are you okay? No, but I'll survive.

And you do. You're soon back on your nimble feet, jumpin' and jabbin'. But you're profoundly different in at least two ways:

1. You will never again go into a corporate mountain pass without first checking for an ambush, and

2. You will do anything to repay that angel, no matter what or where or how much.

It isn't that you saw "I am a traitor" in neon on the departing backs of the others. People shrink from organizational carnage. They don't KNOW what to say and it seems kinder to avoid you. It's that someone was brave enough to stand by you, acid dripping from your soul. You never forget that courage.

Next time you see a work friend fall into a tiger trap or onto her own sword, rush over with outstretched hand. It's the decent thing to do. It's also smart. She'll be grateful to you forever. She will most assuredly be at your side next time (and there will be a next time) your plans become fodder in the mouth of the organizational behemoth.

You can't failure-proof your career, but you'll find—if you've aided a wounded soldier—those hands will help you rise again.

Been there. Bled that.

Winning Strategy #88:

Get up.

Y ou've never felt this bad. You went for the magnificent dream. At first everything went well, a sure sign from the universe that you and your life purpose were in sync.

"Poor fools!" you thought as you watched passersby trudge past your window, despair on their weary faces. while you did your superiority dance. How can they *not* live their dreams, as you've done? Then, the dream becomes a nightmare. *Nothing* goes right. Your decisions stink. Your bank account runs dangerously low, and there are no investors on the horizon. Customers reject your work. Opportunities turn to dust in your hands. Those unfulfilled people on the sidewalk now seem smarter. You're not sure you can go on.

This is a test. Like childbirth's transition phase, it's what you go through giving birth to a dream. In this long, painful, desperate period, the universe tests your desire. You want to flee from the pain.

"What are you willing to do?" the universe asks and tosses thunderbolts of crisis at you.

If you set your jaw, lower your head and muscle on, with fire in your eye, things can suddenly change. The phones ring. Money rolls in. Everybody loves you.

Your sweat and determination were your answer: "I wanted it more than anything." Successful people differ from failures in only one respect: They get up one more time than they fall down.

Get up.

Chapter 7

Leave the Job

We no longer keep jobs for a lifetime. We feel stuck where we are. Something better comes along. We have to leapfrog if we're to work our advancement plans. The awful boss finds a way to get rid of us. We throw off our golden handcuffs and head for the grandkids.

People have between four and seven careers during their working lives. That figure seems unbelievable when you're just beginning and you're sure THIS is the path; and can't conceive of doing anything else because it was so hard getting to THIS job. Change does happen, though; either because life dropped a bomb or a blessing or because you took a look at the path behind you and decided there had to be a better way and set off toward the diverging path ahead.

This chapter is about leaving your job, on your own volition or at someone else's not-so-benign invitation, about getting downsized, or retiring. There are a few things you need to know.

What's the best way to resign?

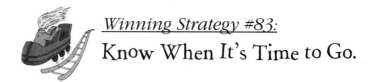

Winning Strategy #83:

Know When It's Time to Go.

We all have bad days at work, creatively dry periods that feel as hot and unnavigable as the Sahara Desert. We moo out the window at others who unquestionable prance to more interesting jobs. We also spend time flipping that old career coin in the air: Stay? Go? But we worry: What if I don't find a job right away? How can I ever make this much money? My family needs this income!

Confounding issues such as that often cause us to rein in the rebellious dreamer within who had stirred things up by gazing longingly at an uncluttered horizon. We decide to be grown-ups and just get back to work.

Sometimes that strategy works, and we apply our "Aye! Aye!" hand to the job that may not thrill us but covers our essentials. Sometimes that urge to go rages in us, but we feel obligated to stay ("The group needs me") or we fear the unknown, so we keep dousing the fire. Guess what? You just THINK you are! If it's really time for you to go, your behaviors show it. Here are some of them:

1. You change from being "On-Time Hal" to "Where's Waldo?" You may have arrived a mere 15 minutes ahead of the get-to-work

gong, now you're slightly late each day. You're also five minutes late for meetings. You miss that important blabfest beforehand where the agenda items really get worked out. You're out the door like a shot at quittin' time. Your sterling attendance record changes. You call in sick every few weeks.

2. You remove yourself from your co-workers. You park at the OTHER end of the lot from the spot you and your pals designated as yours. You no longer lunch with them. You either have errands to run or you plead deadlines and eat at your desk. You quit the bowling team. You feel out of the loop and resentful, and it never occurs to you to see yourself as being the reason.

3. You spend lots of time in the bathroom. Okay, everyone else also takes the *Wall Street Journal* down the hall, but three times a day? Actually, you sit in the stall, head in hand, dreading the walk back to the cubicle with the walls that close in more each day. You straighten your desk 'way too much or not at all, or talk on the phone to friends, or plan unnecessary trips out of town. On a good day, most people are productive about four-and-a-half hours. You're lucky if you get in one or two ripping hours.

4. Your performance slips. You may have always come screaming from the copy room—hastily bound report in hand—just in time for the important meeting, but at least you got it there. Now your monthly reports are late. You screw up a big project. You quit the United Way Committee, having been its prime HOO-rah boy. You contribute little at staff meetings, except to shoot from the hip and dodge your boss' glare because your remarks were superficial or premature or just plain wrong. You don't cozy up to the boss, you play lousy politics, and you don't water your brownie-point plants.

The saddest thing about these signs is that you generally don't recognize them as the beacons they are, blinking the message at you: "It's time to go!" You don't pay attention to your own behaviors, but you start getting sour about everybody else. Why have your friends deserted you? Why is your boss acting like such a jerk? Why doesn't this company do something that HELPS people instead of robbing them blind?

What you're not looking at is these are the same people, boss and products that excited you for so many years. THEY haven't changed. YOU have. The performance slide happens last, but that's when the organization stops worrying about where your usual vim is and starts getting annoyed by you. The performance slip is, frankly, your engraved request asking them to kick you out; in other words, to do TO you what you wouldn't do on your own steam.

How does this dreadful passage proceed? At first, as I said, because you've been a valuable employee, everyone feels concern. Then, when you treat a work friend haphazardly or make the boss look bad, they start to change their opinion about you even though it takes time to reverse a high opinion to a low one. Finally, when it's clear you're no longer on the team, that's when the boss invites you in, closes the door and says, "What's going on here?" If you don't fix it, you've got another few months before the firing machinery clicks to its dreadful close and you're out the door. All told, it generally takes two years from your profound despair to the slamming door.

Can you reverse it? Absolutely. The question is, will you? Will you renew your heart so you're happy at what you're doing? Will you find something outside work that gives you enough satisfaction to make those 8 hours of servitude survivable? It's all doable and it's all up to you. People are happy to change their minds about you, unless you've stepped onto that last slippery slope with a defiant glower and jutting middle finger.

 It's up to you. Just realize that if you're heading down the hall with the newspaper again, it's not a twitchy colon. It's time to go in other ways.

Winning Strategy #90:

Leave like President Nixon.

When people leave jobs, they often write a long letter to the person in charge. It details company flaws, warns of wasted opportunities, or intones what the next person in this job must do to be successful. They deliver it with a serious flourish, as if carrying out a noble duty.

How much does the effort matter? Put together the tip of your index finger and thumb. See the zero? You got it! When you leave, it's as if you pulled a finger from a glass of water. A little ripple, then a smooth surface again. Oh, the farewell party speeches will laud your accomplishments and wonder how the organization will go on, but—in fact—your duchy begins reshaping around you the moment you announce your departure. The focus becomes what the new person will do with the job, not what the leaver thought. Human beings forge toward the future rather than reflect on the past. Companies go on quite well without us. Difficult truths.

The company may want to know why you're leaving, may hold an exit interview, may ask for your recommendations. Give that information, but be succinct. Don't waste your time and psychic energy on wasteful work. It may seem vital to pass along scads of information, but it is usually regarded casually, if at all.

Richard Nixon resigned from the presidency of the United States, one of the most powerful jobs on the planet. Bedeviled by the press for two years after a pre-election Watergate complex break-in sanctioned by his re-election committee, accused by the citizenry of abuse of power, angry at the lack of recognition for his accomplishments on the world stage, and on the verge of impeachment, he had—don't you think?—plenty to say. How did he go? He wrote these 17 words to Secretary of State Henry Kissinger on August 9, 1974:

"Dear Mr. Secretary: I hereby resign the Office of President of the United States. Sincerely, Richard Nixon."

Simplicity did the job for him. It should do the same for you.

Leave like President Nixon.

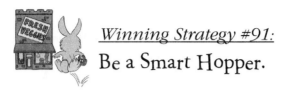

Winning Strategy #91:
Be a Smart Hopper.

When you begin your career, you want to get different experiences, but when should you worry that employers will see you as a job hopper?

That question was easier to answer ten years ago. You were expected to stay at your first job two to three years, the second for two to five; and the third was to last your entire career. Today it's a mixed bag. Some companies or industries follow this same pattern; others have an "up-and-out" philosophy—they only want you for three years; some professions naturally have high turnover rates (like clerical and sales jobs); and companies go belly-up. Unfortunately, people and machines scanning resumes flash "warning" if your Experience section has too few years in a job.

If you have experience patches like that on your resume, tell potential employers you got recruited or took a promotion or got downsized But if you've never held a job for more than 2 or 3 years…honey, you're a job hopper.

What if you HAVE? How can you make your resume look better? Maybe you've had three or four jobs in the same industry. Group those jobs under an industry heading. (But don't do a "functional" resume. Employers will think you're hiding something.) Explain your job history, either on your resume or the cover letter. Best of all, get face-to-face meetings. If they like you, they might overlook your bunny feet.

Then there's the circumstantial hopper, the spouse of someone whose business or military service keeps the moving van fired up every couple of years. Say what you will in an interview, you won't convince anyone THIS is the time you're putting down roots. Sell them on having a wonderful you for two years; say you won't leave till you hire your replacement; but don't count on the offer letter. You will probably have to develop a portable career (a web designer with clients all over the country, a quilt maker) or sign up with a nationwide temp firm, or look for one of those "up-and-out" companies, who want you gone after 24 months.

If you're the third kind of job hopper, an office door swinging shut behind you can feel like cell bars on your restless executive back. You may be a starter, not an implementer. You have kind of a John Wayne thing; you love swaggering into town and rounding up the bad guys, but the day after you dismiss the posse, being the town marshal mostly means putting the town drunk in jail Friday nights to sleep it off. You don't like it when it gets tame or bureaucratic. You have entrepreneurial edges. You get itchy, want to move on.

A time or two you wear out your welcome but don't go, either because you're afraid to 'fess up to your boredom and head out of Dodge on your own steam or you're not aware of yourself as someone who should only have jobs with frequent change on the menu or "John Wayne" in the job description. Sometimes the company eases you out.

Your problem is relatively easy to fix. Just acknowledge yourself as what you are and realize that you need new challenges, you like being a trouble shooter . Only look for those kinds of jobs. Stay in an industry and make yourself known there so the switches at least make sense. You could be happy in crisis- or project-based industries where change is the norm, or in big businesses that frequently transfer employees; which means you'd constantly have a new job.

Don't try to pretend to be someone else and hope they don't see the "hopper" in you. Look for the job that WANTS a hopper.

Can I just quit?

Winning Strategy #92:
Just Quit.

Can you just quit before you have another job? Sometimes:

1. If you feel in danger, either from the physical challenges of the job or the presence of someone who seems threatening...and the organization does nothing to protect you. No job is worth harmful exposure. Because legalities are involved here, however, talk with an employment attorney about when and how to leave.

2. If you've wanted to go for months, but your job demands have kept you from making even the easy contacts. You've made no progress, and each day at work gets harder.

3. If you want to relocate and your next job isn't findable on the Internet or through a recruiter (which means your job isn't in particular demand), or new companies won't relocate you (this is true for lower level and many entry level jobs). It takes twice as long to find a job from another city. It's difficult to get interviews from a distance. Companies want to control recruiting costs, and they'll look locally first, so flying you in is not their Plan A. You don't have the contacts there to facilitate your networking. If the location is your top career priority (oh, those beaches! oh,

those mountains! oh, those Broadway plays!) hitch up the station wagon and follow your star to Dream Land.

4. If you're worn down, frazzled, beat up, and you can't face your 9:00 to 5:00 daymares. You might as well leave, talk incoherently to the walls of your apartment for a few days, get a grip, get up and start looking for the next job. This situation is a ripe breeding ground for the "What happened to Joe's attitude? Let's fire him" bug. If you stay because you're scared to go, the company frequently helps you out the door.

5. If your job will be jeopardized by the hunt's visibility.

6. If you're headed for another career that requires retraining, or starting your own business. What's the point of staying and delaying?

7. If the economy is golden and your next job is as gettable as plucking an apple from a late summer tree.

Before quitting, have a nest egg to tide you over for six months (or the amount of time it'll take to get the next job). You want to know you can cover your living expenses.

What about the gap you'll have on your resume? In some cases there won't be; but generally, the time is quite explainable to the next employer. It represents a blip on your career screen.

It should not be your main career strategy, but sometimes you just have to quit.

Winning Strategy #93:
Leave the New Job You Hate.

Y ou just started a new job and you hate it. Can you leave right away? No, unless you can get your next job TOMORROW. But you shouldn't stay two years to make your resume look good. You would find a thousand ways to make the company fire you long before then: playing computer games, surfing the net or making personal phone calls.

Almost everyone hates the new job the first day or so. Wait a bit. An employment study found it takes 17 days to get accustomed to a new job. Don't be hasty. At the same time be looking around the company to see if different responsibilities or positions exist there. If the company spent time and money to find you, they'll want to keep you, unless the organization is tiny and this is IT in the job department.

Still unhappy? Keep waiting. If it took you awhile to find this job, don't be too eager to jump ship. Instead, do your job by day and your hunt by night. It takes longer to find a job when you have one, so realize you may be there another six months. Be careful, in the meantime, that your dislike doesn't show. The company could invite you to leave, most likely at the end of your 30- or 90-day probation period, when such conversations are typically held.

How did you make such a bad choice? Maybe your spouse insisted, "Just get a job." Or, these could be hard economic times, and no other was around. The biggest reason people choose badly, however, is that—when they went on the interview—they tried so hard to look good they didn't pay attention to whether the company looked good to THEM.

If you've given it your best shot, then leave. To the extent you can, be generous with the employer in giving notice; maybe a few weeks longer than required so they can find your replacement. Leave on friendly terms, if it's possible; and don't feel too guilty. The people in the company probably intuited you didn't feel a fit, even before you did.

What's the best attitude to have
toward the job I'm leaving?

Winning Strategy #94:

Dance with Skeletons.

I was being followed in a job by a close friend. I knew everyone would love her and that she would be better at the job than I, all too aware how much I was leaving undone. When I thought about it, a depressed nervousness sifted over my shoulders.

We had a three-week overlap. It wasn't the chummy sleepover I'd expected. She would snipe at me in meetings, and I wasn't particularly friendly either. Finally, one morning I asked her, "Hey, what gives?"

"I know how much the people love you," she said. "I'm afraid I can't fill your shoes." With that, I brought my skeletons out of the closet (my fears she would harshly judge my half-done projects) and introduced them to my friend. We danced all those worrisome bones into the light of day, which took away the power they'd had over us. The rest of the transition was smooth. And, yes, she was far better at the job.

When you leave a job, you worry about unfinished projects, what people will say about you, especially the ones who dislike you. We forget that, on any given day, a boss could fire us for the work we do (or don't do). We're not perfect, timely, complete. If you're in management, when projects stretch out for months and years, you might not even know on a daily basis if you're doing a good job, even though it's your best.

Additionally, your reasons for leaving this job can add to your inefficiency: Planning the new job, too much work in the current one, being in over your head. Even if you were doing a decent job before, you might not be by its end.

Stop worrying about it.

Leave-taking can be full of surprises. People you never knew liked you will mush all over you. Supposedly good friends will now diss you (it's a way of building scar tissue over their "abandonment" wounds). They WILL discover you were only half as great as you'd pretended to be. And, yes, your detractors WILL talk about you.

 You can't control any of it, so why worry? You won't even be interesting gossip a week after you've gone. Drag your skeletons out, wind up the old Victrola and dance with your bones toward your new horizon. Don't be afraid of what you leave behind.

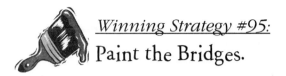

Winning Strategy #95:
Paint the Bridges.

You know the woman in Business Development you hate, the admin who treated you rudely, the manager who took credit for your work? You've waited for today. You're leaving and you're all revved up to tell them what you think. Steam hoots out of both ears.

Stuff it. The warning you've heard about not burning your bridges is right. You don't know when you'll need these people. I don't care if you're leaving for Nepal, vowing never to touch these shores again. The world has gotten too small. You just never know.

I worked for a man who was told by his boss to get rid of me, and he did. I knew what he was doing, and I hated him for it. We later became close friends. It's just the way the world turns. You change. You learn that business and friendships work in baffling ways. You get craftier, but old hurts stop smarting because you let them go. Fate brings you and the nemesis together again. You embrace. You resume with a forgiving heart.

Don't tell people off. It doesn't change anything or make you feel better. Wherever you can, paint the bridge. Keep a well-lighted path between you and the people you're leaving. Most of the relationships will fade. One day, you'll be surprised to see a former enemy picking her way through the brush, eager to find you and to renew, maybe even to apologize (as happened with me and my old boss).

the **Point**

Oscar Wilde said, "A man cannot be too careful in the choice of his enemies." Make as few of them as you can. Concentrate on making friends and on being one. You'll need them all before you're through.

How do I get over being fired?

Winning Strategy #96:
Get out of the Fired.

I am so sorry this happened to you. You walked in this morning and got a call to see the boss. The cold roller-coaster dip your stomach took was your tip-off that nothing good would come from this trek down the hall. Now you sit in your car outside the building, an employee no more. Fired. Stripped of your 9 to 5 identity, with your box of discarded contributions sitting on the seat next to you. Fired.

You will mostly keep on your best face for everyone, maybe even your spouse who will worry about how soon you can replace the income. You'll tell varying shades of the truth about restructuring, mergers, discrimination. You'll act hopeful, upbeat. But your ego has taken a wallop to the middle and is retching on the parking lot. It can be one of life's cruelest blows. This isn't about your competence or whether you'll find another job or make enough money. This knife slices to the core of your self-confidence and, like deep wounds, takes a long time to heal.

Why did this happen? How do you get over the shock and pain? How do you manage the hurt?

1. Why? In a few weeks or months you may be more able to face the "firing" truth. Were you incompetent? In many cases, it isn't

performance. The employer just didn't want you anymore: The new boss didn't like you. The organization was in turmoil and rejected your attempts to fix it. They wanted different ideas. The owner's son is old enough.

Sometimes, though, it IS you: You hated your job but wouldn't leave, so the organization eased you out, having sensed your rejection of IT. You were in over your head. You brought bad habits to your job (late, careless, too disagreeable, too much personal stuff).

It all hurts pretty much the same, no matter the reason. If it WAS you, you may have a hard time taking an honest look at behaviors you need to change; you'll be angry, defensive, blaming. If it WASN'T you, you'll feel wobbly-kneed, unself-confident, depressed.

It CAN happen that you'll feel jubilant (and this is the spin you'll probably put on it), that this is an opportunity to try something new, that you're shaking this old dead place out of your boogie soul.

2. What to do? Decide how long you need to mope. Twenty-four hours? Three or four days? Take it. Be as sad as you are. Wallow in your misery. Sit in your bathrobe and sulk on the back porch. Take long naps with your face to the wall. Don't make networking calls. You have a bit of depression to work through. You might as well get it out of the way.

3. Manage the hunt. Then, on the chosen day, leap from your bed of woe and get to work. If you're being outplaced, go to your new office. Otherwise, give yourself a week to organize your work-seeking life. Get office supplies. Take over the basement or an attic room or a corner of the dining room (no TVs allowed!) for your exclusive use. Scope out the weeks or months ahead and

decide whether you need a fax or if Kinko's will do. Do you need a new desk or a door over a couple of file cabinets? Get your benefits arranged and wrap up details from your old job. Talk with your spouse about how solid the finances are and how you need to live for now. Join a job hunter's club. Make friends with a reference librarian (they are GOLDEN at helping job seekers find career information. They know where to look and they're patient at teaching you.)

4. The search. One of the most sanity-preserving techniques will be your routine. Show up at 9:00 (wherever your "work site" will be). Leave at 5:00. If you're at home, don't do laundry or vacuuming or watch the baby. If you can't ignore the hum of home, then go someplace else.

Decide what you want. A new career? If you don't know what that is, go to Chapter One, but know the search process will be 9 to 24 months. Another job? Get your tool kit in order: (a) What are you looking for? Give it a name. Don't be vague. Your friends can't help with vague. Where? (b) What skills and experience do you bring? Have a list so you can handily recite them in an interview. (c) Why you? An employer will want to know why you're they're best choice. Be specific. (d) Where will you look? Want ads? Internet? Friends? Recruiter? (e) Who do you know? Call them. Tell them what you want. (f) Shape up your resume so you look like the job you're seeking. (g) Start hammering the phones; set up breakfasts, lunches and interviews (and set weekly goals for each). (h) Take one day off each week. This is hard work and you will need a psychic break.

That's pretty much the order, but it takes awhile for most people to settle down to it. HAVING A ROUTINE IS KEY.

5. What to tell people. Be as honest as you can with yourself and your family. With friends, tell them the same thing you'll tell a potential employer. Be brief, though. They love you, but they mostly hate hearing problems like this. They don't know how to help, especially when your response to their help offer is "Yeah, find me a job."

6. What to tell potential employers. You do not destroy your career by getting fired. You DO hurt your chances if you talk about it in the wrong way. Here's how to present it: (a) It was them: "There was bad chemistry between my boss and me." "We had a different philosophy about marketing." (b) It was you: "I spent too much time on personal calls. The experience shook me out of that habit, but that was why." You get points for honesty.

7. The future. You will be different. . .maybe less loyal, more attuned to changes in the political wind, more careful about your work habits.

 **You will get over this.**

Winning Strategy #97:
Stop Getting Fired.

There is a group of people who never hold a job. They operate the machinery called a political campaign. Months before the race they turn up at headquarters as operations directors or budget managers. After the race they land in some vaguely titled job at a company run by a friend of the pol's. When the next run heats up, they're back on the political staff. They raise families; they wear nice suits; they hold their heads high in church. Their resumes look like hell; but their resumes don't matter. The contacts and political value do.

Another group also frequently lose their jobs, but there's no friendly, politically helpful firm to take them in. They get fired or step out just ahead of the firing squad. They tell the little wo(man) or the next interviewer it was the organization's fault. Once or twice, maybe. More than that. . .nope. What's true about them is (pick one or more) they never get along with the team, they think theirs is the only way; they're erratic performers; one day a star, next a bum; they skip a lot of work or come in late; they take care of personal business at work. Drugs and alcohol are often background siren songs.

If these are your termination reasons, you've got some serious changing to do, in attitude and behavior. It's hard to take a brutally honest look at yourself, but it would mend your work life if you could mend your ways.

How? Alcoholism and drug use respond to Twelve-Step programs which emphasize honesty and cleaning up your responsibility act. Immature or puzzlingly stupid behavior often gets helped through the insights therapy provides. Some problems have roots in mental illness, and those can be helped with your determination to work on the illness, your family's support, drugs and therapy sometimes. Whatever your "first cause" is, if you want your life to be different, you have to give up the blame game, acknowledge you have a problem and go seek the help you need. The path will be a challenge, but those who take it say it's worth it.

 Most people have a "fired" or "escorted out" in their background. They just don't talk about it. If it keeps happening, though, ya gotta splash your face with the cold water of "no kiddin'", take a good hard look at yourself and set out to change your ways.

How do I handle being downsized?

Winning Strategy #98:

Get Super-Sized After Downsizing.

The hobnail boots of downsizing wreak emotional havoc. You may get the announcement two years in advance and take up residence on stress mountain worrying if the axe will fall on YOUR cringing neck. Or, one Friday morning, your quivering-voiced boss may tell you, with Human Resources present, the pleasure of your company is no longer required. Here's a phone number of the outplacement service or the un-employment office. Oh, yeah, give us that badge. Shell-shocked, you go to the resume workshop or the outplacement firm.

Here are some downsizing tips:

1. If you get advance notice. Start looking the MINUTE the press release hits the bulletin board. If you're a hotshot the company wants, ask about an incentive to stay; but keep looking. Do your job, but let the loyalty go. Don't spend endless days trying to discern whether it was you; you might not be able to read the tea leaves. Play a balancing game. Be on the team because you need the relationships; still, it's every man for himself. (Stress? Yes!) Forget about productivity, budgets, new ideas, long range plans. Update your skills. Don't work 60 hours a week as the company winnows employees. You'll exhaust yourself, and it doesn't protect your job.

Should you bolt or wait? BOLT if the next job is at hand, if the situation will only get worse, if you can make more money elsewhere. Life's too short to hang onto a bad thing. WAIT if a severance package is coming, if your next job will be hard to find, if you can bear the tension of a sinking ship.

2. If you get last-minute notice. They SAY "downsized." You FEEL "fired," devastated. Take off a few days, but scramble into the job hunt as fast as you can. Form a job club with fellow downsizees or join one. Don't wait till the last two weeks of your severance to search. Build in a break before taking the next job. This has been hard on you, and you won't get a vacation soon.

3. What's next? Is it time for you to make a long-desired change? Do your kids need you more than the snarly customers? Are you finished with the fast track? Do you want school or re-tooling or escape from a failing industry? How might this be an opportunity?

4. In the interview. When the interviewer asks about the downsizing, be careful. If the whole division got wasted, the decision was economic; but if your previous company cherry-picked you, the assumption is "poor performance. " Have a good reason why you were the only programmer out of 20 to go.

5. You will get through this. You will be changed by it. It could happen again, despite your best checking on the company's economic health. It's small comfort, but you'll manage the second or third downsizing with more aplomb and you'll get out of job jail faster. Stay on your networking toes and never again let yourself get blindsided. Stay trained, ready, networked and only loosely loyal so you'll never again get so pummeled.

the Point

If you keep your career flight bag packed and your eye on the horizon, you'll fare better in the next downsizing storm.

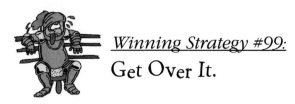

Winning Strategy #99:
Get Over It.

You were a captain of industry, leader of thousands, Pooh-Bah of divisions. The company heaved and you got ho-ed. You got a nice package, a bountiful outplacement service and a 12 x 12 office (with a window!). Things aren't going well. You've looked into several opportunities, but they lacked substance. It's been several months and you can hardly get up in the morning.

What's up?

Your counselors know because they watch how you invite other outplacees in for a morning schmooze, hang on the phone, then leave by noon. They long to help, but you avoid them with a tight smile. This is what they wish they could say to you:

Get over it.

It sounds cruel, considering the blow your psyche has taken. Your self-worth was tied up in those mogul-meetings and marketing victories. You had a structure, position, pride, evidence of never-fail capability, ease, a place to go and problems to challenge your brain and take a whack out of your prodigious energy. Every single bit of that is gone. Your family is there for you, but. . .

You're like the prizefighter who took a sucker punch and went down for the count, whose coach HAS to say, "Get over it. We'll win the next one." There's no point in mollycoddling you or letting you dwell on defeat. How can you win again? You know this game. Get back in it.

Study yourself with your deepest periscope and frankest eyes to know who you are and what you want and what you're in it for now. Drain that counselor of every ounce of competent insight and advice. Keep both hands on your bootstraps, all day every day.

Time is your enemy. Your age, income and status mean you'll take longer to get back on the happy career train. You get older and poorer and less attractive to the business, academic or medical world the longer you delay. Your opportunities don't develop overnight. Are you a turnaround expert? Do you want to buy a company? Does a company want a president? If you've been out of work for six months or more, you are probably flirting with depression; and it only gets worse, not better. Get going.

 You have a hard road to go. Do what your counselor tells you, and order the door hangers out of your office because they're blocking your way outta there.

How should I organize retirement?

Winning Strategy #100:
Do It Early.

He had retired two years previously but was still struggling with the transition from captain of industry to sometime consultant. He had taken a retirement transition workshop two years before his "See ya!" date.

"You know," he told me, "they should have gotten us started at least five years before I retired." His comments included the emotional as well as the financial planning aspects.

Here's what you need to take care of:

1. Beginning. Start early. Like the man said, ten years before you retire, you'd better have the first family planning meeting on the subject. Earlier is even better. There are people who, on the first day of their career, are thinking about the last one. You probably know someone who had a good job but lived simply, saved and invested and then at age 45 said, "I'm done!" That's a rare bird indeed. I hope you DON'T wait till ten years before retirement to begin saving for it, but you'd be shocked to know how many smart people DO.

One reason to start early is what too often happens to people in their 50s. The world and the economy and the work changes, and the highly successful six-figure executive gets dumped and can't even find a job for half that. There are many ways to deal with it, but what if you'd planned on this cushy income and it vanishes overnight, never to return? It happens.

2. Planning. We are diligent oxen, most of us, plodding through the days on a path that gets deeper with each traverse of our field. We plow ahead, looking neither left nor right, habituated to the task, chewing our cud with more or less content. We are into our routine. We do not plan. When we reach a time of profound change without a plan, it's as if we heaved ourselves against a door we expected to be stuck, but it flings open at our slightest touch and we tumble-bug through it.

A few people wear themselves out on the corporate treadmill, and after the cake and party they sling golf clubs over their shoulder and never look back, never give that place a second thought. They had a plan.

3. Financial. Read books. Meet with a planner. Many experts will tell you you'll need an income approximately the same for five-plus years after leaving your job. Can you afford to retire? What will you get from pensions, 401(k)s, investments? Will you still need to work?

Live like you know you'll have less income rather than pushing your credit card limits.

4. Family. Do your in-town kids want you to be a "granny nanny"? Do YOU want that? Do the far-flung ones want to see a LOT of you? What does your spouse expect of you? ("I married you for better or worse, but not for lunch"). Will your spouse still work? Will you drive alone on that R.V. trek you intend to take around the country?

5. Social. Do you have younger or older friends? Do you want to be in an adult community, or do you love to have babies on your knee? Do you want to retire elsewhere? Do you want to stay in that big old house, or does a freedom-giving condo look good to you?

6. Mental. What will you do to keep the neurons firing? How will you keep from being the crabby revisionist that no one at the party wants to talk to? What language have you always wanted to learn? What books have gone too long unread?

7. Idealism. Have you been wanting to give back? Does a not-for-profit want you for staff or board? Do you want to start an outreach program for your church? Will you go on a mission to a third world country to build housing?

8. Career. You may not be finished working, whether or not you want to be. The statistics say we're retiring earlier, but that we get tired of golf after about five years. We want to work; we may also need the money. And we're healthy enough to work past age 65. Will you be happy as a Wal-Mart greeter? Does a small, worthy organization want you as a three-day-a-week controller? Are you eager to spend more time on the antiquing sales that took up your weekends? Do you want to teach? Go back to the beginning of the book and do some of the career-change exercises.

9. Emotional. What will you do without the money, status and power, or other symbols of the job that took up your day, gave you your identity? What will you call yourself now? What will bring meaning to your life?

the Point

These are not easy questions. Take time to work through them and include your family. You'll be spending lots more time with them. They matter.

Afterword

I hope you've found a strategy or two that helps you avoid a career blunder or solve a vexing problem. You have undoubtedly sensed what my philosophy is relative to people and their jobs.

1. Know who you are and what you want.

2. Be guided by what feels right to you.

3. Be willing to ask wise others for help and work hard to recover from troubles.

4. You'll be better for the struggle.

5. Accept responsibility for all of your journey and all that you are... the great and almost-great.

A second hope is that you have the courage to go for what feels meaningful to you, the humor to know we're all blundering through the same awkward life dance, and the grace to step into success and arise out of failure.

Call me if I can help.

The Next 100 Winning Strategies

Volume 2 is already underway. Do you have a burning career question that didn't get answered here, and you believe the next Job Doctor book should address it? Send your suggested questions to JobDoc@aol.com

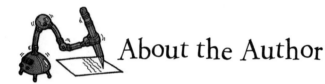

About the Author

Rose Jonas is "TV's Job Doctor." She regularly gives career advice on television and radio news programs. She also gives workshops and speeches on careers, especially how to get smarter at the career game.

As a career counselor, she works with career changers, job seekers, and people trying to get out of "career jail" (bad boss, pressure to leave, unfair treatment). As President of The Jonas Company and an executive coach, Rose helps client companies solve strategic and people problems: employment, career development, strategic planning and team building.

Rose has a Ph.D. in Human and Organizational Systems from The Fielding Graduate Institute. She received a fellowship from the Coro Leadership Training Program. Rose is a trained Gestalt therapist, and is certified as a career coach and in the Myers-Briggs Type Indicator.

"TV's Job Doctor" is available as a speaker and workshop leader. You can reach Rose at 314.863.1166 or JobDoc@aol.com

 # Cool Career Books

These are books clients tell me helped them:

Bridges, William, *Managing Transitions: Making the Most of Change*, Addison-Wesley Publishing Company, Inc. 1991.

Cameron, Julia, *The Artist's Way: A Spiritual Path to Higher Creativity*, G. P. Putnam's Sons, 1992.

Chapman, Jack, *Negotiating Your Salary: How to Make $1000 a Minute*, Ten Speed Press, 2001.

Frankl, Viktor E., *Man's Search for Meaning*, Simon & Schuster, 1984.

Knowdell, Richard L., *Building a Career Development Program: Nine Steps For Successful Implementation*; Davies-Black Publishing: Palo Alto, CA, 1996 $18.95

Lakein, Alan, *How to get Control of Your Time and Your Life*, New American Library, 1996.

Lore, Nicholas, *The Pathfinder: How to Choose or Change Your Career for a Lifetime of Satisfaction and Success*, 1998.

Machiavelli, Niccolo, Translator George Bull, *The Prince*, Penguin Books, 1962.

Porot, Daniel and Haynes, Frances Bolles, *The 101 Toughest Interview Questions...and Answers That Win the Job!*, Ten Speed Press, 1999.

Porot, Daniel and Bolles, Richard Nelson, *The PIE Method for Career Success: A Unique Way to Find Your Ideal Job*, Jist Works, 1995.

Rosner, Bob; Halcrow, Allan and Levins, Alan S., *The Boss's Survival Guide*, McGraw-Hill, 2001.

Rosner, Bob, *Working Wounded: Advice that Adds Insight to Injury*, Warner Books, 1998.

Sher, Barbara, and Gottlieb, Annie, Wishcraft, *How to Get what You Really Want*, Ballantine Books, 1979.

Sinetar, Marsha, *Do What You Love, the Money Will Follow: Discovering Your Right Livelihood*, DTP, 1989.

Stein, Marky, *Fearless Interviewing: What to Do Before, During and After an Interview*, Writers Club Press, 2001.

Tieger, Paul D., and Barron-Tieger, Barbara, *Do What You Are: Discover the Perfect Career for You Through the Secrets of Personality Type*, Little, Brown and Company, 1992.

Too, Lillian, *Feng Shui Fundamentals: Careers*, Element Books Limited, 1997.

Acknowledgements

This book began in Dallas, Texas, when my niece, Julie Finkelstein, pelted me with questions about her looming post-college career.

"There oughta be a book," I said, "to give you fast answers to your basic questions." Julie said if I wrote it, she'd buy it. I promised her a fabulous family discount. Thanks, Julie, for inspiring this book.

Then there are the clients whose lives, dreams and misadventures endlessly fascinate and inspire the topics. We've walked miles together. You have no idea what a gift you are to me. I include most especially the Monday morning breakfast club, you hardy souls who braved the dawn after my TV gig to schmooze, plan, razz, cheer and otherwise help each other over your respective career shoals.

I owe a particular thanks to Ava Ehrlich who, as executive producer of Channel 5, promoted the idea of creating a Job Doctor to help people through the 1991 recession and believed in me. Jennifer Blome and Art Holliday are extraordinary anchors whose patience, tolerance, intelligence and humor make them favorites with their millions of viewers. . .and me. Producers Jim Williams, Danita Blackwood, Stephanie Zoller, Greg Harris, you taught me lots. And to the whole "Today in St. Louis" crew - Scooter, Robin, Ron, Andy - thanks. You all had a turn at telling me my mike was off, "Don't wear that color!" my make-up looked lousy, or "Hey, you were funny today."

Then there are my readers, generous souls who picked at my writing bones, gave me tough advice, kept me on target and accountable. I owe you, big-time: Donna Bridgeman, Jan Cerny, Jim Dowd, Ruth Finkelstein, Melissa Fox, Kate Gibbs, Nancy Gucwa, Kristin Koppen, Paula Kosin, Ray Jaeger, Andrea Rosen, Rochele Santopaulo, Donna Sarro, Ellen Sweets, Carol Weisman, Jim Williams.

Particular thanks go to Bonnie Miller, attorney, who managed this feckless writer and the project itself; Jeff Michelman, lawyer to the stars; Georgia Ellis, cheerful assistant.

Husband Ed and son David gave me the time and space to chase a muse and gnash my teeth, and forgave me when I got lost in the concept and had dinner delivered...again.

Notes: